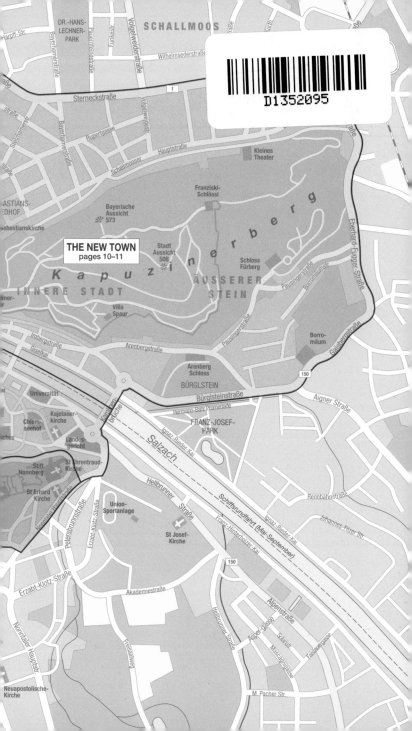

INSIGHT GUIDES

SALZBURG

smart guide

APA PUBLICATIONS

Part of the Langenscheidt Publishing Group

Contents

Areas

A–Z

Below: windows on the Mozart Geburtshaus.

Left: looking over the city from the Mönchsberg.

Below: *tracht* for sale on Getreidegasse.

3

Salzburg

Founded on the wealth from salt mined from the neighbouring mountains, Salzburg is a Baroque jewel set in beautiful Alpine scenery. An Unesco World Heritage Site, the attractive old centre is dominated by the Hohensalzburg fortress that towers above the city. The birthplace of Wolfgang Amadeus Mozart, it is also the venue for a world-famous music festival.

Salzburg Facts and Figures

Population of city: 150,300
Population of region: 530,000
Highest point in city: the Kapuzinerberg at 636m (2,087ft)
Highest point in region: the Grossvenediger at 3,674m (12,054ft)
Year ceded to the Austrian Empire: 1816
Year the city centre became an Unesco World Heritage Site: 1996
Oldest Unesco World Heritage Site in province: the Hallstatt salt mines, formed 230 million years ago
Lowest point in the region: the Traunsee at 191m (627ft), the deepest lake in Austria

History and Heritage

Few towns depend so much on their heritage for income as modern Salzburg, but the history which suffuses every breath and step taken in this city's streets and its province's hills is a complex one which merits closer attention. Behind the apparently uncomplicated facades of Austrianness, Mozartmania, Catholic tradition and provincial pride lie centuries of conflict and ambivalence which survive as the shadowy side to any twee touristic depiction of Salzburg. Despite its representation as quintessentially Austrian, the city is in fact only a late addition to the Austrian lands, being acquired by the Habsburgs in 1816 after the Congress of Vienna, and despite the stirring tale of the Von Trapps, Austrians have had to acknowledge their role as perpetrators as well as victims of Nazi persecution.

The region's roots as a settlement lie in various communities of the Stone Age, the first existing on the Rainberg and surrounding plains. During the subsequent Bronze Age, copper mining established Salzburg as a vital part of the Central European economy, although deposits of salt – 'white gold' – came to be more valuable during the era of Celtic domination in Europe now known as the Hallstatt culture, after the Salzburg town which left the greatest archaeological legacy among its peers.

Austria was overrun by the Roman Empire around 15 BC. The Celtic kingdom of Noreaia was renamed Noricum and was allowed limited self-government for half a century before Roman strategic concerns led to militarisation of the province. Rome kept up a lively trade with all corners of its empire, and with Noricum sitting on the Danube the province was of key importance. During this period, Juvavum – today's city of Salzburg – was established at the meeting point of three key roads.

Gastfreundlichkeit and Manners

Much has been written of the Austrian tradition of *Gastfreundlichkeit*, or hospitality, over the years. At the 1815 Congress of Vienna, which redrew the map of post-Napoleonic Europe, diplomats accused the Austrian hosts of attempting to gain political sway

Below: rock salt for sale.

through overly seductive hospitality. To this day foreign travellers find this a pleasant country in which to travel. The people are unfailingly polite and hospitable, which is hardly suprising given its dependence on the tourist industry, and this goes a thousandfold for Salzburg. Although a relatively late addition to Austrian territory, only incorporated at the start of the 19th century, the city has quickly come to epitomise its motherland's orderly and gracious nature.

Hand in hand with Salzburg's devotion to hospitality and politeness goes a certain rather formal insistence on good manners. In this regard, playing to Austrian snobbery works wonders for the independent traveller. Those of a scruffy appearance may be banished to pensions distant from the sights by tourist information staff, but the mere addition of a buttoned down shirt evokes a totally different response. While it is commonplace to suggest that the young are more open, progressive and easygoing in this regard, in fact with the first postwar generation entering retirement, age is no longer a predictor of any given Austrian's attitude to social nicety. Indeed, Austrians are like people the world over; some friendly, others less so. The main difference between this nation and others is that while a friendly Austrian will of course be welcoming and helpful, an antagonistic one will simply become sniffily, but still unfailingly, polite.

Highlights

▲ **The Festung Hohensalzburg** Towering above Salzburg, the castle of the Archbishops has shaped the history of the city.
▶ **The Festival** Founded in 1920, this is one of the world's greatest festivals of music and drama.

▲ **Hallstatt and Dachstein** This region, with its Celtic heritage and wonderful scenery, is an Unesco World Heritage Site.

▶ **Caves and Mines** The region is honeycombed with huge mined and natural caverns, many of which can be visited.

▲ **The Grossglockner Hochalpenstrasse** With views of Austria's highest mountain, this road winds through spctacular scenery.
▶ **Hellbrunn Palace** Trick fountains and wonderful decoration.

The Mönchsberg

Salzburg's central mountain, the Mönchsberg (literally the 'monk's mountain'), stands at 503m (1,650ft) and dominates the Altstadt. Quite apart from the huge Festung Hohensalzburg, residence of the Archbishops of Salzburg, the forested top gives spectacular views over the city and surrounding mountains and is one of the nicest places to stroll away from the busy streets below. Also here is the city's Benedictine convent and the Museum of Modern Art. At the northern end of the mountain is the one-time village of Mülln, now absorbed into the city, with its delightful church and brewery.

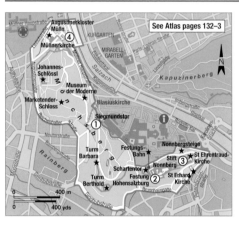

Above: a wreath adorns the door of the Müllnerkirche.

The Ascent

There are a number of ways, with varying degrees of effort, to 'climb' the mountain. The most popular by far is to take the funicular railway (the FestungsBahn) that runs from Festungsgasse straight into the heart of the Festung Hohensalzburg (the price of the ticket is included in the entrance fee to the fortress). This precipitous ascent provides good views, but if you do not have a head for heights it might make you a little queasy.

If you are heading for the fortress and would rather make the ascent on foot, a series of stairways starts

The main collection of Salzburg's **Museum der Moderne** (Museum of Modern Art) was moved into a new building on the Mönchsberg in 2004. As well as the collections it has a lovely café and restaurant with views over the city. The easiest way to reach the museum is by the lift at Gstättengasse 13. *See also Cafés and Bars, p.36; Museums and Galleries, p.98*

nearby and runs up by the ramparts to the entrance. Two more stairways can be taken from this side of the Monchs-berg: the first, Nonnberg-steige, lies to the east and runs up from Kaigasse to the

Nonnberg Convent; the second lies at the eastern end of the Festival Halls, in Toscanini-hof, where a somewhat forbidding stairway has been cut into the dark rock, bringing you out to the west of the Festung Hohensalzburg.

A further way up on foot can be made via a series of stairways from the other side of the **Siegmundstor** ① tunnel (take the footpath to the right of the tunnel entrance when coming from the Altstadt). This was cut through the narrowest part of the Mönchsberg in 1764–7. Alternatively you can wind your way up through a series of defensive gateways from Mülln and walk the length of the mountain on forested trails to the fortress at the far end.

Left: the Festung Hohensalzburg stands proud above the city.

abbess. It is the oldest convent to exist without interruption in the German-speaking countries. Hence, only the church and the Chapel of St John can be visited.

Descending along Nonnberggasse and Erhardgasse you will come to the quiet, Biedermeier-style Nonntaler Hauptstrasse. On Erhardplatz is the church of **St Erhard**. Built in 1685–9 by the architect Johann Caspar Zuccalli, the stuccoed interior has a notable altar painting by Rottmayr (1692).
SEE ALSO CHURCHES, P.56

Mülln

The **Müllnerkirche** ④ is a late-Gothic buttressed church (1439–53) with a stuccoed interior dating from 1738. It once belonged to an order of Augustinian hermit monks. A staircase to the left leads down into the vaulted cellars of the **Augustiner-Bräustübl**, a brewery with a popular beer garden. Within the grounds of the nearby **St Johanns hospital** is a church (1704) designed by J.B. Fischer von Erlach.
SEE ALSO CAFÉS AND BARS, P.36; RESTAURANTS, P.108

The Festung Hohensalzburg

The city's **fortress** ② and citadel has stood on this rock since the time of the Romans. Work on the defensive complex that stands today was initiated by Archbishop Gebhard (1060–88), after he had taken the pope's side against the emperor in the Investiture Dispute. The fortress was built because Gebhard needed a means of defence against attacks by the troops of those who had remained faithful to the emperor.

The fortress's present appearance is largely the result of building activity under Leonhard von Keutschach (1495–1519). Since the archbishops were not only churchmen but also powerful temporal rulers, they frequently needed the fortress as protection against forces from outside and revolts within their own territories. The fortifications that ring the Mönchsberg were so strong that the fortress was never taken by force.
SEE ALSO CASTLES AND PALACES, P.42

The Nonnberg

The eastern end of the Mönchsberg is known as the Nonnberg. The **Stift Nonnberg** ③ was founded in around 700 by St Rupert, who appointed his niece, St Erentrudis, as the first

Below: the arms of the archbishops of Salzburg in the Hohensalzburg Fortress.

The Altstadt

A long with the buildings on the Mönchsberg, the old city of Salzburg has been declared a World Heritage Site by Unesco. Characterised by atmospheric narrow roads and passages that link squares dominated by wonderful Baroque churches, the Altstadt (or 'old town') is where Mozart was born and where the festival started in his honour has its concert halls. Trapped between the Mönchsberg and the Salzach river, this compact district can feel a little swamped by tourists, but the crowds are soon forgotten as you peer into shop windows, tuck into delicious local food and explore the Altstadt's museums and churches.

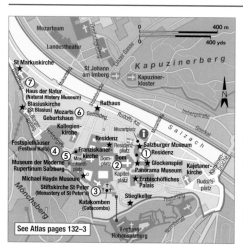

Above: atmospheric back-streets at dusk.

Mozartplatz

At the eastern end of the Altstadt is the square that celebrates Salzburg's most famous son, **Mozartplatz**. In the centre of the square is a statue of the composer. On the northern side is the main tourist information office through which you can book tours and accommodation. Facing the office is the large **Salzburg Museum** in the Neue Residenz (enter through the courtyard) dedicated to the history of the city.

SEE ALSO MONUMENTS, P.94; MUSEUMS AND GALLERIES, P.100

Residenzplatz

The large square that leads off from Mozartplatz is **Residenzplatz**. The large building that sits on the western side of the square is the **Residenz** ① itself, the town palace of the prince arch-bishops. Passing through the imposing entrance brings you into a large inter-nal courtyard. From here you can visit the state rooms, while on the upper floors is the **Residenz Gallery**.

The southern side of the square is faced by one side of the Dom, but its centre-piece is the splendid Resi-

denzbrunnen. This Renais-sance fountain was built by Tommaso di Garona in 1656–61. To the east is the **Glock-enspiel**, the tower of the Neue Residenz that contains a carillon of 35 bells. It plays tunes, some by Mozart and Haydn, daily at 7am, 11am and 6pm. Also tucked away on the side of the Neue Resi-denz is the **Panorama Museum**, with a selection of the large paintings so popular in the 19th century. You can get tickets here to see the workings of the Glockenspiel.

SEE ALSO MONUMENTS, P.95; MUSEUMS AND GALLERIES, P.100

Left: the Kollegienkirche with the Dom behind.

church, while in front of you, laid out along Hofstallgasse, are the **Festspielhäuser** ④, or 'Festival Halls', the main venues for the Salzburg Festival.

Across the square is the **Museum der Moderne Rupertinum Salzburg** ⑤, an annexe of the Museum of Modern Art on the Mönchsberg, and the rear of the Kollegienkirche, built by J.B. Fischer von Erlach in 1707.
SEE ALSO CHURCHES, P.57–8; FESTIVALS, P.69; MUSEUMS AND GALLERIES, P.98–9

The Getreidegasse and Mozarts Gerburtshaus

Universitätsplatz at the front of the Kollegienkirche is linked to Salzburg's main shopping street, **Getreidegasse**, by a series of interesting passages, now lined with expensive boutiques. On the main street is the **Mozarts Gerburtshaus** ⑥, where the composer was born.

At the far end of Getreidegasse is the Gothic church of **St Blasius**, once a hospice. Further on, on Anton-Neumayr-Platz, is the **Haus der Natur** ⑦, the natural history museum, behind which is the **St Markuskirche**.
SEE ALSO CHURCHES, P.58; MUSEUMS AND GALLERIES, P.99

Below: a memorial in St Peter's cemetery.

The so-called **Katakomben**, or catacombs, that are cut into the cliff face in St Peter's cemetery are in reality three early-Christian cave chapels. At some point they may have also served as retreats for the monks of St Peter's. *See also Churches, p.58*

Dom- and Kapitelplatz

Domplatz lies off Residenzplatz and this rather tightly enclosed space is dominated by the façade of the **Dom** ②, Salzburg's cathedral. The first cathedral was built in 767–74 by St Virgil, and was replaced in 1181, but this second church burned down in 1598. The Italianate structure now in place was designed by Santino Solari and the cathedral was rededicated in 1628. The western front is the venue for the performance of Hofmannsthal's *Jedermann* ('Everyman') that starts each Salzburg Festival.

The last in this series of squares is Kapitelplatz, which is on the south side of the Dom. The entrance to the Festungsbahn is nearby, and also here is the **Neptune Fountain** erected by Anton Pfaffinger in 1732 on the site of an old horse pond.
SEE ALSO CHURCHES, P.56; MONUMENTS, P.95

St Peter's and the Festspielhäuser

The cemetery of the **Monastery of St Peter's** ③ leads off from Kapitelplatz. This is the oldest Christian burial ground in the city. The monastery church is an interesting mix of Romanesque and Baroque architecture.

The exit at the far end opens into a series of linked courtyards, between which is the **Michael Haydn Museum**, and then into Max-Reinhardt-platz. On the right is the tall **Franziskaner-kirche**, a Romanesque and late-Gothic

The New Town

The Staatsbrücke ('State Bridge') over the Salzach leads visitors to Salzburg's New Town, as the sector to the north-east of the Salzach or 'Right Bank' is commonly known, although it is only 'new' in relation to the Altstadt. This brings you to the Makartplatz, an important hub for buses. It is, however, the Mirabell's flower gardens which epitomise Salzburg's New Town; fragrant, colourful, manicured to within an inch of its life but with such love and care that it retains the power to charm even at its most stylised. Also on this right bank is a good pedestrianised shopping area and some of the city's coolest bars.

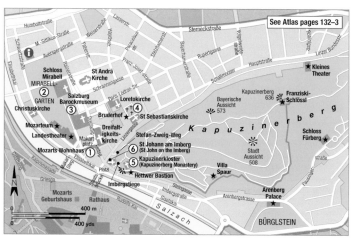

See Atlas pages 132–3

Makartplatz to Schloss Mirabell

Although **Makartplatz** is an attractive square, with a beautiful garden overlooking the **Mozarts Wohnhaus** ① and the **Dreifaltigkeitskirche**, the Makartplatz has a tendency to feel throttled by traffic at busy hours of the morning and afternoon. Nonetheless, many stoic Salzburgers enjoy spending an hour on its benches in the sunny weather.

The **Schloss Mirabell** may not be fully open to the public, but its gardens now form one of the most spectacular parks in Salzburg, with their fountains and seasonally replanted flower beds. A large area of the **Mirabellgarten** ② is given over to a park, characterised by the strong scent of its many pine trees, which includes a restaurant, playground and, for those seeking a quick dip, a spa named after Renaissance healer **Paracelsus**. The space was originally designed by the favoured architect of 17th-century Austrian princes, Fischer von Erlach.

Caspar Gras' statue of Pegasus will prove particularly

Left: the Mozart Wohnhaus.

Left: the beautifully manicured Mirabellgarten.

Off Linzergasse lies the **Bruderhof**, a quiet little courtyard with a US/Italian-style café, wine bar and glittery furniture on sale at **Desiderio**. This cool, cobbled corner is where Salzburg's classy (and wealthy) young things go.

Passing the Stations of the Cross, chapels and a crucifixion group (1780) you will arrive at the **Kapuzinerberg Monastery** ⑤. The **Hettwer Bastion** gives wonderful views over the city.

Descending via the Imbergstiege you pass the little church of **St John on the Imberg** ⑥ (1681). The narrow Steingasse snakes along the Kapuzinerberg. Many of the tall houses here date from the Middle Ages. The road eventually becomes the Arenbergstrasse and leads to the Biedermeier Arenberg Palace. Between 1912 and 1922 it was the home of the Austrian dramatist and novelist Hermann Bahr. Since 1968 it has been the home of the Max Reinhardt Research Institute. SEE ALSO CHURCHES, P.59; LITERATURE AND THEATRE, P.90; WALKS, P.128

The New Town contains a number of significant castles, including the **Schloss Mirabell**, the **Schloss Fürberg** and the **Schloss Arenberg**. *See also Castles and Palaces, p.44–5*

iconic for fans of *The Sound of Music* – it is here that Maria teaches the children to 'Do Re Mi' their way to happiness. Georg Trakl's poem *Musik im Mirabell* on the north wall of Mirabell garden conjures up the sounds of the park. The gardens also host the **Salzburg Barockmuseum** ③ (Baroque Museum). SEE ALSO CASTLES AND PALACES, P.45; CHILDREN, P.54; CHURCHES, P.59; FILM, P.72; MUSEUMS AND GALLERIES, P.100; SPAS, P.118

The Pedestrian Zone

The principal street of the pedestrian zone is Linzergasse, which runs down to the riverside Platzl, a tiny square

of courtyard cafés and shops which is met by the eastern end of the Staatsbrücke.

Turning off Linzergasse it is possible to find respite from the city bustle in the **Cemetery of St Sebastian** ④, where pines and mausoleums nestle within a tranquil colonnade. While it is the mausoleum of Prince-Archbishop Wolf Dietrich which forms the focal point of the cemetery, other historical celebrities resting here include Mozart's father and widow, as well as the alchemist Paracelsus. SEE ALSO CHURCHES, P.59

The Kapuzinerberg

To climb the **Kapuzinerberg**, Salzburg's highest point (636m/2,086.6ft), take the short, steep path named after Stefan Zweig, which begins beside the gateway of the house at No. 14 Linzergasse. The writer lived in Paschinger Mansion (Kapuzinerberg 5) between 1919 and 1934.

Below: St John on the Imberg.

Around Salzburg

The French cultural critic Roland Barthes once wrote of French travel guides that when the writers used the word 'picturesque' they meant 'hilly'. The reverse is true of Salzburg and its surrounding countryside: if the landscape is hilly, it is truly picturesque… and the Salzburger Land is very, very hilly. It is hard to say whether this seduction is purely due to some innate power of landscape over the human soul, or rather the successful, decades-long marketing of the Austrian countryside from 19th century travel guides to *The Sound of Music*. In either case, to be in Salzburg's immediate surroundings is a truly moving experience.

See Atlas pages 134–5

South of the City

Schloss Hellbrunn ① was built as a summer residence by Prince-Bishop Marcus Sitticus. It lies beyond the city limits in the countryside, but can quickly be reached from the town centre on bus No. 25. Alternatively, walk along the traffic-free Hellbrunner Allee. Bordered by 300-year-old trees, this runs from Freisal Palace in the Nonntal past a number of other palaces and mansions to Hellbrunn.

Apart from the 17th-century Italianate palace with his beautiful frescoes, the main attraction is the gardens with their surprise fountains. On Hellbrunn Mountain you will also find the **Monats-schössl** (1615), now the **Volks-skunde Museum** (folklore museum). The Stone Theatre (probably the oldest open-air stage in the region) is said to be where the first opera was performed in the German-speaking world in 1617. Also nearby is **Zoo Salzburg**, where most animals are kept in large, open-air enclosures.
SEE ALSO CASTLES AND PALACES, P.46; CHILDREN, P.55; MUSEUMS AND GALLERIES, P.101

AROUND THE UNTERSBERG

Hangar-7 ② near Salzburg airport not only houses the Flying Bulls collection of vintage aircraft, but also holds art exhibitions. It is a rather strange combination of architectural elegance, engineering museum, a café and art gallery. Close by is another museum, **Stiegl's Brauwelt**, set in the brewery of the popular local beer.

Anif, 6km (3.7 miles) south of Salzburg, is famous for its 16th-century reconstructed neo-Gothic moated castle (privately owned and closed to the public), which is surrounded by landscaped gardens. The Austrian conductor Herbert von Karajan, who lived here, is buried in the village cemetery.

Above: the Open-air Museum.

At the western foot of the Untersberg is the **Salzburg Open-air Museum** ③ at Grossgmain, where 40 historic farm buildings from the Salzburg region have been reconstructed with great care.
SEE ALSO CAFÉS AND BARS, P.41; CASTLES AND PALACES, P.46; CHILDREN, P.55; MUSEUMS AND GALLERIES, P.100–1

North of the City

There are also a number of short excursions to the north of the city, all reachable by regular bus (check www.post bus.at for times and frequency) or, for Oberndorf, S-bahn (www.oebb.at) services.

Left: a *tromp l'oeil* fresco in the Schloss Hellbrunn.

me in those days where Paradise was, I would have answered without hesitation…right by the Wallersee.'

The Benedictine abbey of **Michaelbeuern** ⑥ is easily reached by bus from the stands outside the railway station in Salzburg. It is thought to have been founded in the 8th century and received many later additions. As well as an important library it has some fine Baroque paintings.

The two villages of **Arnsdorf** and **Oberndorf** have gone down in history as the birthplaces of the carol *Silent Night*. It was written in the former by Franz Xaver Gruber. However it was first performed in Oberndorf, until 1816 a suburb of Laufen, which lies in Bavaria on the opposite bank of the Salzach. A chapel and museum celebrate the event. Also here is the Baroque pilgrimage church of St Mary.
SEE ALSO CHURCHES, P.59; MONUMENTS, P.97

Maria Plain ④ (1671–4), situated 5km (3 miles) north of Salzburg, is a pilgrimage church built by court architect Giovanni Antonio Dario from a commission by Archbishop Max Gandolf Kuenberg. Mozart's Coronation Mass is performed here every year on the Feast of the Assumption (15 August). You can pick up the footpath following the Stations of the Cross at the Plainbrücke (Lokalbahn train S1 or S11, then a 30-minute walk).

A direct bus runs from Mirabellplatz to the pretty village of **Mattsee** ⑤. Set on the eponymous lake, the village itself lies on a spit of land which separates the Mattsee (also Niedertrumer See) from the Obertrumer See. It is thought the **monastery** here was founded by Duke Tassilo of Bavaria some time after 777. Close to the monastery is the Schloss Mattsee, which in parts dates back to 1100. It is now used as a conference centre and for wedding receptions (www.schloss-mattsee.at).

South of Mattsee is the **Wallersee** where the German dramatist Carl Zuckmayer lived from 1926–38. He was lavish in his praise of this spot, writing in his autobiography, 'If anyone had asked

> If I have neither the inclination nor the experience to climb Salzburg's local 'proper' mountain, the **Untersberg** (1,853m/ 6,079ft) on foot *(see Walks, p.128)* then you can take a cable car to the summit. Bus No. 25 goes to the bottom station in the village of Grödig (www.unters bergbahn.at; daily, times vary but generally 8.30am–5pm, closed for maintenance end-Mar and Nov). At the top, apart from the stupendous view, is a restaurant and a series of rocky footpaths (wear sensible shoes) on which you can explore the limestone summit.

Below: the altar at the abbey of Michaelbeuern.

Hallein and Berchtesgaden

To the south of Salzburg lie two rather different towns. Hallein is noted for its medieval streets and beautiful Baroque houses, as well as a world-class museum showcasing the area's Celtic heritage. On the nearby Dürrnberg is one of the region's most interesting salt mines, with a history reaching back to the time of the Celts. Berchtesgaden, actually just over the border in Germany, is set in the most spectacular Alpine scenery and will be of great interest to historians of the Third Reich.

See Atlas pages 136–7

Hallein

Hallein ① is the second-largest town in the province of Salzburg, the district capital of the Tennengau and an important industrial centre. Easily reached by train from Salzburg 15km (9 miles) away, it has an attractive town centre surrounded by the remains of the former fortifying walls. The centre of the town is largely traffic-free; many of the streets date from the Middle Ages and are bordered by houses with colourful Baroque and rococo facades.

A large paper mill is the town's main employer, but in former years salt mining brought wealth to Hallein. Salt was discovered on the Dürrnberg by the Celts, and was mined there as recently

as 1989. Until the early 1990s, the town's Perner Island was an industrial site with a large salt processing plant, but it has now been turned into a cultural centre and every year stages a number of performances during the Salzburg Festival.

The parish church of **St Anthony the Hermit** was rebuilt in 1965–6. Franz Xaver Gruber was organist and choirmaster here. His grave is the only one to have remained when the adjoining cemetery was cleared away. To the north of the church you can also still see the house in which he lived.

The town's main attraction is the **Keltenmuseum** and a further insight into the world of the ancient Celts can had on the town's mountain, the **Dürrnberg**. There is a road

leading up the mountain but you can also ascend by cable car; the valley station is on the southern edge of town. Here is the **Hallein salt mine**, now open for tours. Included in the price of the ticket is the open-air Celtic Museum, a reconstruction of a farmstead complex and a grave. A Celtic information trail completes the exhibition.

SEE ALSO CAVES AND MINES, P.53; MUSEUMS AND GALLERIES, P.101

Berchtesgaden

Just 30km (18.6 miles) south of Salzburg, across the border in Germany, is **Berchtesgaden** ②. Trains run from Salzburg to Berchtesgaden and buses link the town with the village of Obersalzberg nearby. Alternatively, during the summer 'Eagles Nest Tours' run from Mirabellplatz

Right: the Keltenmuseum is modern and well displayed.

Left: the wonderful setting of the Königsee.

reach the Eagle's Nest, a remarkable feat of engineering. From the upper bus stop, a lift takes you 124m (406.8ft) to the house itself.

Berchtesgaden, like many other places in the area, also has a disused salt mine that has now been turned into a museum.
SEE ALSO CAVES AND MINES, P.53

Königsee

To the south of Berchtesgaden, and within Germany's Berchtesgaden National Park, lies **Königsee** ③, one of the most beautiful lakes in the region. The narrow fjord-like lake runs 9km (5.6 miles) north–south in the shadow of the Watzmann, its giant east face rising almost straight out of the water. From the small village of Königsee, at the northern end of the lake, during the summer you can take a boat trip along its whole length. You pass **St Bartholomä**, where there is a curious Baroque church with twin onion domes, and finish at **Salet**, the lake's southern tip. In order to preserve the lake's environment the tourist boats are electric and other boats are strictly limited.

The hills around Berchtesgaden make a surprise appearance in *The Sound of Music*. As Salzburg is close to the German border, the Von Trapps could not have hiked to freedom over the mountains to Switzerland; in reality, they took a train to Italy. The final scenes of the movie in fact show the actors walking in the direction of Hitler's 'Eagle's Nest'.

in Salzburg's New Town (www.panoramatours.com). Set amid beautiful Alpine scenery dominated by the impressive peaks of Germany's second-highest mountain, the Watzmann (2,713m/8,900ft), this delightful little town encapsulates all the attractions of the Bavarian Alps, including painted houses, a little royal palace and wonderful views.

However, the area has a darker side. **Obersalzberg**, just above the town, was where in 1934 Hitler bought a chalet known as the Berghof. Here he entertained his friends, Nazi Party functionaries and, in 1938, Neville Chamberlain, the British prime minister. A Gestapo headquarters was established nearby, and beneath it all was a network of underground bunkers.

Most of these buildings, including the Berghof, were destroyed in an Allied air raid in 1945, and the remains were blown up by the West German government in 1953. You can still visit the **Kehlsteinhaus** or 'Eagle's Nest', commissioned by Martin Bormann as Hitler's 50th birthday present from the Nazi Party although, due to his fear of heights, it was little used by the Führer (daily mid-May–Oct; entrance charge; www.eagles-nest.de). Perched on the summit of the Kehlsteinberg at 1,834m (6.017ft), a bus runs up on a road built specifically to

Below: walking through Hallein's salt mine.

The Salzkammergut

Not a province in its own right but nonetheless one of the mostly distinctive regions of modern Austria, the 'Salt Chamber Estate' which stretches from Upper Austria through the Salzburger Land to Styria has been shaped by two kinds of 'white gold'; the glacial ice which carved its characteristic lakes and the salt which has been mined since the time of the ancient Celts. Today's Salzkammergut presents a delightful contrast to the provincial capital of Salzburg which, although hardly touched by smog or pollution, cannot compete with the fresh air of the mountains and the clear fresh water of the lakes.

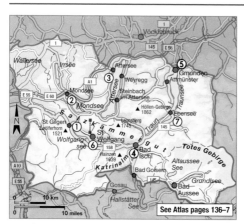

See Atlas pages 136–7

Above: Mozart's mother was born in St Gilgen.

Early Tourists

While a number of salt mines are still active today in the region, and some have even opened their doors to tourists and travellers, the principal attractions of the present-day Salzkammergut – watersports, hiking, skiing and historical spa towns – arose during the late 19th century. It was during this period that the imperial Habsburg nobility acknowledged this 'earthly paradise' among their possessions and the Salzkammergut came to be favoured by figures from Kaisers and Tsars to Freud, Schubert and Schönberg as the Austrian resort region par excellence.

St Gilgen

St Gilgen ① marks the gateway to the wider region of the Salzkammergut, but it is often visited as a swift (45 minutes) day trip out of Salzburg, buses departing from Mirabellplatz. The town alternates between preternaturally peaceful moments (arrive before 10am and you will probably hear only the sound of your own footsteps in the streets) and a bustle of diners, tourists, travellers and sports fanatics. The church, with its distinctive onion-shaped domes, is a little way from the lake and gives focus to the town's centre, dotted with hostels, hotels, restaurants

and *Kaffeehäuser*. Among visitor attractions are the **Museum der Völker**, dedicated to musical instruments from around the world and the **Zinkenbacher Museum**, celebrating the artists' colony which once existed here.

St Gilgen's Busbahnhof might seem rather optimistically named, given that it is an unstaffed, prefabricated shelter, however, the Postbus service is in the process of building a full station over the coming years. Until then, travellers awaiting their connecting service can take warmth and sustenance from the small café at the cable car station a short walk away. Alternatively, ferry services exist between St Gilgen and its rival tourist town, St Wolf-

which is a publicly owned and maintained bathing area with its own promenade. Further inland, a number of attractive cafés adorn the **Marktplatz**, or market square. Very much a resort town – and a sporting resort at that – Mondsee is best visited in the high season when its attractions are at their peak, although even in quieter months and less clement weather its shoreline provides a pleasant spot for idle leisure. **St Michaels church**, which hosted the wedding of Maria and Captain von Trapp in the film version of *The Sound of Music*, is also notable for the altars sculpted by 17th-century artist Meinrad Guggenbichler.

Buses arrive at a rather unprepossessing site a short distance away from the shops and amenities, but five minutes' walk brings you to the pastel paradise of the town centre. While the town is well-served from Salzburg, buses from St Gilgen to Mondsee are few and far between, with connecting services sometimes many hours apart.

SEE ALSO CHURCHES, P.59

Below: the Church of St Michael, Mondsee.

It was three 'miraculous' births that gave Bad Ischl its pre-eminent reputation among Austrian spa towns in the 19th century: Franz Josef and his two brothers were the 'Salt Princes' who were born to Sophie von Habsburg after an 1828 visit to Bad Ischl seemed to cure her diagnosed infertility.

---

gang, on the opposite side of the **Wolfgangsee** or take the 4- to 5-hour walk around the lake shore.

The nearby **Zwölferhorn** peak can be reached by cable car, the station conveniently located adjacent to the bus stop. The staff are very friendly and offer safe storage of luggage too bulky to take to the summit; just ask at the counter. The cable cars, constructed in 1957, seat four and offer a breathtaking 15-minute ride each way. If you stop here between the hourly buses

from Salzburg to Bad Ischl there is just time to ascend and sample a quick coffee and strudel at the excellent and aptly named Café Panorama before the next departure. Those with a little longer to spare may ascend to the very peak of the mountain, marked by a cross, although care must be taken on the deceptively easy-looking paths; although the mountain is well-tended, there is little direct supervision of walkways and proper footwear is essential.

SEE ALSO MUSEUMS AND GALLERIES, P.102–3; WALKS, P.129

Mondsee

The shores of this crescent-moon lake provide the best sailing and windsurfing in the country. In addition to numerous boat-hire huts and the largest water-skiing school in the country, the shores of the **Mondsee** ② host a **Seebad** (lake bath) on the waterfront,

Attersee

The **Attersee** ③ is the largest of the Salzkammergut lakes (20km/12.4 miles long, 3km/1.8 miles wide and up to 171m/561ft deep). The lakeshore has long bathing beaches and little villages are dotted along the edge. In the south, the Attersee is framed by the Schafberg massif, the Leonsberg (1,745m/5,725ft) and the steep Höllen-Gebirge (1,862m/6,109ft); in the north, they fall away less steeply. Many tools and pile dwellings from the Stone Age have been found here. Signs of Roman occupation have also been discovered, including villas in **Weyregg**.

The hill on which the church stands forms the centre of the village of **Attersee**. It was formerly the site of an early medieval imperial palace. Between 1721 and 1728 the count of Khevenhüller had the castle chapel rebuilt, transforming it into the Baroque parish and pilgrimage church of **Our Lady of Attersee**. Below the church is the lakeside promenade.

Bad Ischl

Narrow streets make **Bad Ischl** ④, a little spa town favoured by the Kaiser, seem deceptively bustling. Accom-

Below: maintaining the Schafbergbahn.

> Above the Ebensee and accessible by cable car, the **Feuerkogel** and **Alberfeldko-gel**, two peaks which stretch above 1,500m (4,921ft), offer the keen walker extensive trails and fine views of the lakes.

modation and food offer good value which will come as a pleasant surprise to those accustomed to Salzburg prices. Here the Habsburg motto k.u.k. – *kaiserlich und königlich,* (imperial and royal) – is rendered as *Kur- und Kaiserstadt,* the imperial spa town, and the distinctive yellow of the Habsburgs is the tone of choice for many buildings' paintwork. The **Kaiservilla** itself is open to the public and well worth a visit.

More Habsburg mementoes can be found in the **Stadtmuseum Bad Ischl**, which also houses a wide range of national and regional costume. The local summit is **Mt Katrin**, some 1,500m/4,921ft high and furnished with downhill pistes and trails appropriate for hiking in summer or cross-country skiing in the winter months. Buses run from the railway station to the cable cars, and are preferable to the short but rather uninspiring walk through the town to the base of the mountain. The tourist office, close to the railway station, is friendly and offers good advice, bike hire, convenient (if somewhat expensive) Internet access, maps and guidebooks (www.badischl.at).
SEE ALSO CASTLES AND PALACES, P.47; MUSEUMS AND GALLERIES, P.103

Gmunden

The banks of the lake and Traun river lend a spacious air to **Gmunden** ⑤, a placid resort town, which earned its

historical prosperity from the salt trade, like many local towns, before coming to rival Bad Ischl in its popularity with the great and the good of imperial Austria. More recently, the town has won fame for the appearance of its 15th-century island castle, the **Seeschloss Ort**, as the backdrop to a long-running television soap opera.

Gmunden's central square, which is home to the town hall and a charming ceramic glockenspiel, faces onto the river and has a number of appealing cafés and well-appointed hotels. Art is sometimes exhibited along the lakefront; otherwise, there are the marina and the swan populace to entertain a lazing eye. Trams, synchronised with the train timetable, operate from the station to the town centre, leading 2km (1.2 miles) downhill through the wreath of retail parks common to most European cities before arriving in

Left: looking out from the Traun Valley.

Bad Aussee, a busy mining town, crosses into the territory of the Austrian province of Styria at the eastern end of the Salzkammergut. Here the devotion to traditional dress is at its strongest, with *Dirndl* and *Lederhosen* giving a pleasingly anachronistic air to streets otherwise swarming with Audis and shoppers. The **Salzbergwerk Ataussee**, used to store treasure by the Nazis and once again devoted to salt mining today, is the main attraction for tourists.

The town of **Ebensee** ⑦, on the southern shore of the Traunsee, offers little to tourists by comparison with its larger neighbours. Even the working salt mine here is here purely for industrial ends. However, the presence of a concentration camp on this site in the later years of World War II make this a significant stopping point. The complicity of Ebensee residents in the work of the concentration camp has left its mark on this small Salzkammergut community, and this shows in the excellent **KZ-Gedenkstatte Zeitgeschichle Museum**.
SEE ALSO CAVES AND MINES, P.52; MUSEUMS AND GALLERIES, P.102

the beautifully maintained centre. Within this zone however, there is the **Gmundner Keramik** factory shop, which has its own stop on the tramline and may be worth a visit.
SEE ALSO CASTLES AND PALACES, P.48

St Wolfgang

St Wolfgang ⑥ lies on the eastern side of the **Wolfgangsee**, opposite its rival St Gilgen (reached by the footpath that begins on the Mondseestrasse). The westernmost village might win out on proximity to the provincial capital, but many regard St Wolfgang as the livelier and more attractive option of the two resort towns. Named for a 10th-century Austrian bishop who saw the site as a rural retreat (and who would probably have been driven from today's town by the sheer bustle and density of souvenir shops lining its narrow streets), the principal attractions for the contemporary visitor are the parish church and the **Schafbergbahn**, a mountain railway which permits an ascent in old-fashioned 'nostalgia trains' that run throughout the day in high season. The journey leads to an 1,800-m (5,905-ft) summit, well-equipped with dining facilities and views of no less than three Salzkammergut lakes.
SEE ALSO CHURCHES, P.60; WALKS P.129

Smaller Lakes

The **Gosausee** is only a minor lake of the region but the Gosaukamm mountains which overlook it are amongst the highest and most breathtakingly impressive of the Salzkammergut, reaching some 2,500m/8,202ft. A cable car ascending from Gosau village will take you as high as 1,500m/4,921ft, offering excellent views and a number of hiking paths.

Below: the pretty centre of St Wolfgang.

Hallstatt and Dachstein

Within the Salzkammergut, the Hallstatt-Dachstein region forms an Unesco World Heritage Site, both for its outstanding natural beauty and features and its significance to early European culture. Hallstatt's legacy to modern archaeology has been such that the town has lent its name to the pre-Christian Celtic culture, characterised by its use of iron, which stretched from Austria into the Iberian peninsula. The town itself is chocolate-box pretty, curving around the edge of the lake.

Hallstatt

Hallstatt ① must be one of the most spectacularly sited towns in Austria, perched on the very edge of the Hallstätter See. The town, although very busy in summer, is usually quiet until mid-morning and there is little point arriving at an overly early hour, except for the most driven of hill-walkers. The boat ride across from the train stop is a wonderful experience, offering the best views of the lake and mountains as the narrow shoreline means the bordering inclines seem to plunge into the water itself. Ask the ferry operators about the lake

excursions which they operate in fine weather during the tourist season.

The boat disembarks at Landungsplatz, the aptly named 'landing square' from which one can turn left for the town proper, or right for one of the many possible

ascents to the church, a must-see for its **Beinhaus**, or 'bone house', a collection of decorated skulls at once macabre and kitsch. At the Landungsplatz, there is also local jewellery for sale adjacent to the ferry station. A café captures tourists' attention after they reach dry land, with a range of gifts, souvenirs and even bags of premium Meinl Kaffee. Order a 'Harbour Coffee' here and you will be given the mug you drank from as a souvenir. The **town museum**, attractive and ultra-modern, merits a visit, its multimedia and interactive exhibits suitable for

Left: in the ice caves.

Obertraun

Hallstatt's lakeside neighbour Obertraun is most famous for the **Dachstein Ice Caves** ② which lie in the mountains above it. The caves form the village's main attraction, and can be visited without difficulty in a day's trip, but there is also a wide range of accommodation available in the town. The train service with Hallstatt and Bad Ischl offers the most reliable and regular service, but the village can also be approached by bus or, most excitingly of all, by boat across the lake from Hallstatt in high season.

Obertraun also plays host to the bizarre 'Five Fingers' installation, a steel platform in the shape of a hand jutting out 4m (13ft) from a 400-m (1,312ft) summit to offer a dramatic vantage point overlooking the area designated as a UNESCO World Heritage site. The walk to the 'Five Fingers' takes just 15 minutes and is far from strenuous; follow the signposts marked 'Pionierkreuz' out of the town centre. The installation is lit for visitors' convenience until midnight.
SEE ALSO CAVES AND MINES, P.50

Below: riding on the Dachsteinbahn.

The themed trail 'Painters, Literati and the Wonder of Nature' runs into the heights overlooking Hallstatt and its lake. A well-marked circular trail of approximately 4km (2.5 miles) – allow up to 3 hours, given the 600m (1,968ft) ascent involved – it passes the impressive Waldbachstrub waterfall, as well as its many lesser cousins.

---

entertaining the youngest of family members as well as those with a more nuanced and developed interest in the region's history.

The excellent displays show how the danger posed by frequent avalanches and landslides ultimately led the Celts of Hallstatt to abandon the settlement and its valuable mines to subsequent generations. These **mines**,

Left: Hallstatt and the Hallstätter See.

still active today, can be visited on a guided tour. This combines a rather theatrical presentation of history with more authentic delving into the galleries themselves.
SEE ALSO CAVES AND MINES, P.51; CHURCHES, P.60; MUSEUMS AND GALLERIES, P.103

LOCAL TRANSPORT

For those unwilling or incapable of the necessary exertions to reach those attractions in the higher reaches of the town, 19th century Hallstatt offered sedan chairs borne by 'Sesselträger'; in 1866, observer Friedrich Simony was just one of those to express great sympathy for those who were expected to carry the very portliest of the great and the good up to the summit. Nowadays the town's funicular railway offers a more reliable (and less exploitative) mechanised alternative.

The Lammertal
and Lungau

South of the Salzkammergut is a spectacular region of high mountains with sheer sides of rock and deep fertile valleys. The province's 'Dolomite Road' runs through the Lammertal beyond which is the 1,740-m (5,709-ft) Tauern Pass that leads over into the remote Lungau region. Here are a string of wonderful castles and Gothic churches as well as pretty mountain villages where people still preserve a traditional way of life. The mountains also supply innumerable opportunities to ski, climb, walk or go rafting.

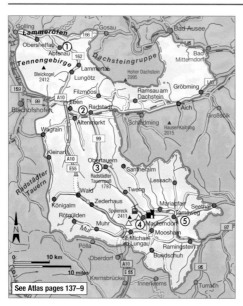

See Atlas pages 137–9

The Lungau is noted for its festivals. *Prangstangen* (poles up to 6m (19.6ft) long wound round with garlands of flowers) are carried into the church in a procession. They remain there as a symbol of life until the Feast of the Assumption. In some villages, the Samson Procession is held on the Feast of Corpus Christi or on a specific day in June or July. A tall wooden statue dressed in armour and a tunic is paraded through the streets. In his hand, the figure clutches the jawbone of an ass, with which Samson is said to have slain the Philistines.

'Dolomite Road' and the views of craggy, whiteish jagged peaks certainly support the comparison.

Before the road begins to climb the Tauern Pass you enter **Radstadt** ②. The circular town wall with its three watch-towers (16th century) is still virtually intact, as is the original street layout. However, due to fires, only one house (Hoheneckgasse 6) and the Romanesque and Gothic church of Our Lady of the Assumption, are still standing. A late-Gothic light column (1513), known as the Cobbler's Column, stands in the graveyard.

The Lammertal

From Golling (see p.24) a road leads east into the **Lammertal**, the most spectacular section of which begins past Ober-scheffau. Here is the entrance to the **Lammeröfen**, a remarkable gorge 2km (1.2 miles) - long and 60m (197ft) -wide. Popular with rafters, there is also a well-constructed footpath along the overhanging rock walls, in some places very close to the water.

Abtenau ① a little further on is noted for its sports facilities. As well as offering water-sports, there are some 100km (62 miles) of marked footpaths and in winter it becomes the most popular centre in the West Dachstein ski region.

The 'Dolomite Road'

East of Abtenau, the road turns southwards. This section through the Lammertal is known as Salzburg's

ing-point for walks and the Speiereck-Grosseck ski area.

Beyond is **Mariapfarr**, the sunniest place in Austria. The village can also lay claim to the oldest church in the Lungau to be listed in historical records (923).

SEE ALSO CASTLES AND PALACES, P.49; CHURCHES, P.60

Tamsweg to St Michael

Tamsweg ⑤ is the regional capital of the Lungau. Thanks to its corner towers, the town hall (1570) on the market place may look like a miniature castle, but was in fact previously a townhouse. The former palace of the Kuenberg family (1742–9) lies in the Kirchengasse, as does St Barbara's Hospital. Originally built as a home for elderly and sick miners, today it houses the Lungau Regional Museum. Also well worth a look is the **Church of St Leonard**.

Beyond Tamsweg is **Moosham** with its impressive **castle**, and further on still is **St Michael im Lungau** with its remarkable concentration of **churches**. This is good starting point for walking in summer and skiing during the winter.

SEE ALSO CASTLES AND PALACES, P.49; CHURCHES, P.61

Obertauern

A former Roman road follows the Taurach Valley before climbing up to the Tauern Pass (1,740m/5,709ft). Near the top you reach **Obertauern** ③. Built as a resort, the lack of buildings of architectural merit is of little concern to the countless holidaymakers who come for the skiing. The border of the Lungau runs through Obertauern. The high-altitude basin is surrounded by mountain peaks and is accessible only via Styria and the Mur Valley.

Into the Lungau

The other side of the pass descends to **Mauterndorf** ④. The name of the village reveals the fact that the settlement had the right to levy tolls (from 1143), making it the oldest customs post in the eastern Alps. It lies on

what since Roman times had been one of the important trade routes to Italy. In 1217 the village also acquired market rights. The townhouses with their stepped gables (16th–17th century) surrounding the market place bear witness to the prosperity this brought. The town is also well-known for its **castle**.

To the west of the village is a cable car leading to the Speiereckhütte, a good start-

The Salzach and High Tauern

The south-eastern part of Salzburg Province follows the course of the Salzach River. Hemmed in by the Kitzbühler mountains and Pinzgau to the south it is characterised by high Alpine scenery, with numerous waterfalls, especially those at Golling and Krimml, and attractive towns, many of which double as winter sports resorts. The valleys and gorges that lie off the main course of the Salzach are equally beautiful and are the location of a number of spa towns and health resorts.

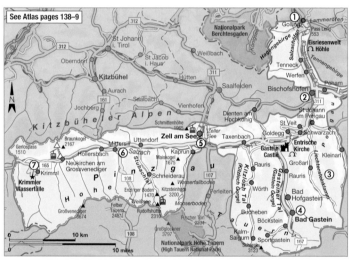

See Atlas pages 138–9

Golling and Werfen

The pretty village centre of **Golling** ① attracts many visitors, and has a number of little gardens on the pavement, locally known as *Schanigärten*. The interesting Folklore Museum is in the castle (the oldest sections date from the 13th century). To the southwest, in the district known as Torren, stands the former pilgrimage church of St Nicholas. Here, too, you

Left: the Cross of St Rupert, Bischofshofen.

will find the entrance to the valley where the Golling waterfall cascades over a 76-m (249-ft) precipice.

South of Golling the Salzach Valley suddenly becomes much narrower. The old Roman Road goes over the Lueg Pass (553m/1,804ft). Here the river has buried itself deeply between the Hagen Mountains and the Tennengebirge, forming the **Salzachöfen**, a gorge some 1.5km/1 mile long, accessible via a footpath leading down from the Lueg Pass.

Left: the beautiful falls at Golling.

bask in sunshine from morning till evening. The principal villages are Schwarzach and St Veit. **Goldegg**, in particular, has a pretty location on this mountain terrace, lying on the shores of a moorland lake (with therapeutic baths) setting off its **castle** to perfection.
SEE ALSO CASTLES AND PALACES, P.49; CHURCHES, P.61

The Kleinarl and Grossarl Valleys

The holiday and winter sports resort of Wagrain lies 8km (5 miles) east of St Johann. It marks the beginning of the **Kleinarl Valley**. Walking up from the Jägersee, said to be bottomless, gives a lovely view of the Tappenkarsee.

The **Grossarl Valley** lies 5km (3 miles) south of St Johann. Its entrance is guarded by the mighty ramparts of the **Liechtensteinklamm** ③, one of the most impressive gorges in the entire eastern Alps. The path through the gorge, which in some places is only 2m (6.5ft) wide ends beside a 50-m (164-ft) high waterfall.

Below: the Liechtensteinklamm in the Grossarl Valley.

In the winter many towns in the region turn into ski resorts, and those that are particularly notable are: Bishofshofen, St Johann im Pongau, Wagrain, Dorfgastein-Grossarl, Schlossalm- Stubnerkogel, Kaprun-Zell am See and the Hochkrimml-Gerlosplatte. *See also Sport, p.121*

Set on the steep rocky outcrop (680m/2,232ft) at **Werfen** in the Salzach Valley to protect the Lueg Pass, the **Eriebnisburg Hohenwerfen** is one of the finest castles in the province. Also close by are the **Eisriesenwelt Caves**, thought to be the world's largest ice cave network.
SEE ALSO CASTLES AND PALACES, P.49; CAVES AND MINES, P.50

Bischofshofen and St Johann im Pongau

Bischofshofen ② lies straddled across the hollow in the Salzach Valley between the mouth of the Fritzbach and the Mühlbach. The region has been settled since Neolithic times. In 700, St Rupert founded a monk's cell dedicated to **St Maximilian** which became the parish church. Also of interest in Bischofshofen are the Kastenhof, a Romanesque residential tower standing beside the parish church, and the Gothic church of the Virgin Mary, also built round an originally Romanesque structure.

St Johann im Pongau was destroyed by a fire in 1855, but no expense was spared with the reconstruction. The heart of the new settlement is a massive neo-Gothic church. Constructed in the historic style, it was nicknamed the **Pongau Cathedral**.

A few kilometres south of St Johann, the Salzach Valley bends to follow an east–west direction, which means that the villages on the southern edge of the Dienten Mountains

The whole region has many fine walks and mountains to climb, some of which should only be attempted by experienced mountaineers and in the company of a guide. Notable excursions include: from the Moosboden Reservoir, the Grosses Wiesbachhorn (3,564m/11,693ft), the Hoher Tenn (3,368m/11,050ft) and the Hohes Riffl (3,338m/10,951ft); from the Hopfelboden car park in the Obersulzbach Valley a two- to three-day tour via the Berndlalm (1,515m/4,970ft), across the Postalm to the Kürsinger Hütte (6 hours), 4 hours further on you will reach the summit of the Grossvenediger (3,675m/12,057ft).

The Gastein Valley

The **Gastein Valley** has enjoyed a degree of celebrity since the Middle Ages. Its gold mines have long since closed down, but the healing powers of the mineral springs continue uninterrupted. The Gasteiner Ache completes its turbuelent course towards the Salzach as it rushes through the **Gastein Gorge**. Perched up above the medieval **Klammstein Castle** and not far to the south stands the **Entrische Kirche**, one of the largest stalagmite caves in the Central Alps.

Bad Hofgastein and **Bad Gastein** ④ are well-known as spa resorts, rising to promi-

nence during the second half of the 19th century, when it was discovered by the Habsburg and Hohenzollern dynasties. The town itself is also an attraction, having grown up around the mighty waterfall of the **Gasteiner Ache**.

Another spa town, **Böckstein**, lies in the upper reaches of the Gastein Valley. The pilgrimage church here of Our Lady of Good Counsel was built in 1764–6.
SEE ALSO SPAS, P.119

The Rauris Valley

Also joing the Salzach, the **Rauriser Ache** (like the Gastein) has to squeeze its way between high rock faces, passing the **Kitzloch Gorge**, which has a waterfall and stalagmite cave. Gold mining was once important in the Rauris Valley, and 15th- to 16th-century workers' cottages can be seen in **Rauris**. The Museum of Local History is set in the former schoolhouse (1563). The parish church has a tower and choir dating from late Gothic times (1510–16), while the nave was built in 1774–80; St Michael's Chapel was built in 1497.

In Wörth, the valley forks into two. A medieval mule path leads along the Seidlwinkl Ache to the Hochtor (2,575m/8,448ft). In the Hüttwinkl Valley you reach Bucheben in 5km (3 miles),

with its parish church and neighbouring priest house (both built in 1785). In Kalm-Saigurn at the far end you can explore the mining ruins along the **Tauerngold Circular Footpath** (3 hours).

Zell am See and Kaprun

Zell am See ⑤, the district capital of the Pinzgau, became a popular summer resort after the construction of the railway line at the end of the 19th century. The town's location on the alluvial headland jutting out into the lake and the walking country were the main attractions. Even Emperor Franz Josef climbed to the top of the **Schmittenhöhe** (1,965m/6,447ft), the famous lookout mountain. Today a cable car provides an easier approach. The town began during the 8th century as a monk's cell, as its name indicates. Three buildings rep-

Left: Pinzgau meadows.

The Felbtauern Road

Mittersill ⑥ marks the beginning of the Felbertauern Road leading towards East Tyrol. Here you can see **Mittersill Castle** (16th century), the parish church of **St Leonard** (1747–9) and the church of **St Anne** (1751). In adjoining Felben the **Felber Tower** (12th-century residence of the rulers of Felben) houses the **Museum of Local History**.

Neukirchen am Grossvenediger lies clustered at the foot of 13th-century Hohenneukirchen Castle (now an old people's home), surrounding the massive Gothic tower of the parish church. To get a view of the Grossvenediger take the **Wildkogel cable car** from Neukirchen to the Braunkogel (2,167m/7,110ft).

Krimml

Krimml is the site of the **Krimml Waterfalls** ⑦. The Ache cascades a spectacular total of 380m (1,247ft) over three rock sills down into the Salzach, one of the highest in Europe. On the road out of Krimml lies the toll station for the **Gerlos Pass** (1,510m/4,954ft), which leads through the high Kitzbühel Alps into neighbouring Tyrol.

SEE ALSO WALKS, P.128

resent what is left of the old heart of the town. **Rosenberg Castle** (1583) is the town hall today, whilst the **Bailiff's Tower** – an old defensive tower thought to date from the 13th century – houses the **Museum of Local History**.

Close by is the resort village of **Kaprun**, the entry point to the Kaprun Valley. Not far from the village is the valley station of the **Maiskogel cable railway** (830m/2,723ft). From the mountain station (1,550m/8,934ft) there is a fine panorama, which takes in the Grossglockner. Even better is the view from the Kitzsteinhorn (3,200m/10,499ft), which can be reached via cable cars from a number of points in the valley. Further on, from Kesselfall House, a post bus runs to the Lärchenwand funicular. Once you reach the top, a shuttle bus reaches the Wasserfallboden (1,680m/5,512ft) and Mooserboden Reservoirs (2,040m/6,693ft).

Uttendorf and the Stubach Valley

Uttendorf is a little village, adorned by a late Gothic parish church and the Gothic church of St Margaret (with a Romanesque core and frescoes). This is the starting-point for a side trip into the **Stubach Valley**, 17km (10.5 miles) long and framed by mountains forming part of the High Tauern National Park.

From the Enzinger Boden (1,470m/4,823ft) you can ascend by cable car to the Rudolfshütte (2,310m/7,579ft). Two glacier nature trails begin here (both 3 hrs): one leads along the south shore of the Weissee and on to the Stubacher Sonnblick-Kees (2,500m/8,202ft); the other towards the Eisbodenlacke (2,070m/6,791ft) and the Ödenwinkel-Kees (2,150m/7,054ft). The Medelzkopf cable car goes even higher to the mountain station at 2,550m (8,366ft).

Below: Krimml Falls.

The Mühlbach Valley

The panorama of the Dienten Mountains, especially the great mass of the Hochkönig, and the Steinernes Meer forms the central attraction of the Mühlbach Valley. It is advisable to choose a fine day for this trip so that you can enjoy the views and make good use of your camera. It is not all scenery, however. The remains of the area's industrial past can be seen in Mühlbach and there are a number of very fine churches, including one with the tallest spire in the province of Salzburg at Maria Alm am Steinernen Meer. At the far end of the valley is Saafelden, a fascinating small town set amid spectacular mountains.

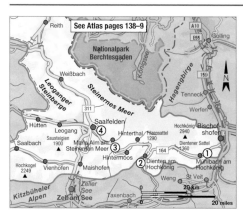

Above: a wall painting, Maria Alm am Steinernen Meer.

Mühlbach

Close to Bischofshofen, the Mühlbach Valley opens up. Copper was mined in the town of **Mühlbach am Hochkönig** ① itself until 1977. The Mining and Local Heritage Museum, with its own copper mine, provides an insight into this former industry (Thur–Sun 2–5pm; www.bergbau-museum.sbg.at; entrance charge).

The Hochkönig

The imposing limestone massif of the **Hochkönig** (2,940m/9,646ft) includes a glacial plateau. It is easy to view the steep slopes of the mountain at close quarters, since you can travel directly

up to the Arthurhaus (at 1,500m/4,921ft) by post bus or by taking the Hochkönig shuttle bus, which runs between Bischofshofen and Saafelden. You can walk from here to the Mitterfeld-Alm (1,650m/5,413ft) in an hour. The ascent to the Matras-Haus (2,940m/

A legend relates the origins of the name of the Hochkönig's glacial plateau, the Flooded Meadow. In order to punish the wanton inhabitants of these rich pastures, who lived in luxury but refused a beggar a piece of bread, a thunderbolt struck the fertile meadowland and covered it with ice.

9,646ft) on the Hochkönig should only be attempted by experienced, well-equipped walkers in good weather conditions (it takes a further 5 hours).

Dienten

Crossing the Dientener Sattel (1,360m/4,462ft) you will come to **Dienten am Hochkönig** ②. The little parish church of **St Nicholas** (1506), with its Baroque onion tower, is perched so picturesquely on a hill that it almost verges on the kitsch. The interior has the double nave typical of the churches of mining communities; collect the key from the priest's house to view the church.

Saalfelden

Saalfelden ④ lies in the Saalach Valley on the edge of the Zell Basin, framed by the Leoganger Steinberge and the Steinernes Meer on one side, and the Kitzbühel Alps and the Dienten Mountains on the other. Thanks to its location, the area has been settled since prehistoric times. In more recent years the town became the administrative centre for the county of Unterpinzgau.

Two fires in 1734 and 1811 destroyed the old buildings. Worth visiting, however, is the **Pinzgau Museum of Local History** in Ritzen Castle (1604), which contains, along with other exhibits, the largest collection of Christmas cribs in Austria. Lake Ritzen's bathing beach is just one of the places where swimming is possible in summer. Still inhabited is the **Rock Hermitage of St George** (1664) above **Lichtenberg Castle** (13th–19th century), northeast of Saalfelden. The town is also home to the longest summer toboggan run in Europe (1,600m/5,249ft).

Maria Alm am Steinernen Meer

Continuing over the Filzensattel (1,290m/4,232ft), you will shortly reach **Maria Alm am Steinernen Meer** ③. The eponymous church is famous for its very tall spire. Between the end of the 14th century and the beginning of the 16th century, churches with lofty spires were built all over the region surrounding Salzburg: in Vigaun, Pfarrwerfen, Altenmarkt, St Veit, Bischofshofen, Hüttau, Mariapfarr, Felben near Mittersill and Maris Alm near Saalfelden.

Pilgrims coming in former times to the church are said to have prayed to the Gothic portrait inside for relief from a plague of bears. Today, such assistance is no longer necessary; wild animals voluntarily keep at a safe distance since the area between Mühlbach and Saalfelden has developed into a skiers' paradise. Politicians and rich industrialists are particularly attracted to Maria Alm and the neighbouring skiing villages of Hintermoos and Hinterthal. Walking, in spectacular scenery, is possible at all times of the year.
SEE ALSO CHURCHES, P.61

The Grossglockner Hochalpenstrasse

The Grossglockner Road is in every respect the most dramatic of all the panoramic routes through the eastern Alps. Initial plans for a road across the Alps had been drawn up at the end of the 19th century, but it was not until after World War I that they actually became concrete. The commencement of the work was postponed several times for lack of funds, but the project finally went ahead in 1924, led by the engineer Franz Wallach, and was completed in 1935.

See Atlas page 138

A toll road, the Grosssglockner is officially open from the beginning of May until the end of October. The opening times are May–mid-June: 6am–8pm, mid-June–mid-Sept: 5am–9.30pm, mid-Sept–Oct: 6am–7.30pm, but sometimes summer snowfalls can close it for days at a time. Before you set off, it is worth checking with the Ferleiten Information Point (tel: 06546-650; www.grossglockner.at) whether the road is actually open or not. The ticket you buy at the toll booth gives you access to the road's exhibitions and sights. The milestones along the panoramic section of the Grossglockner Road measure the distances from Bruck.

Bruck an der Grossglocknerstrasse

The Grossglockner Hochalpenstrasse ('high Alpine road') starts in the centre of **Bruck an der Grossglocknerstrasse** ①. The parish church is neo-Gothic in style and was rebuilt following a fire in 1868–9. It contains a statue of the Virgin Mary which is believed to have miraculous properties and, according to legend, mysteriously arrived in Bruck by floating down the Salzach on an ice floe. The pilgrims' invocation was, 'Mary on the ice floe, protect us from danger as we go'.

Fusch an der Grossglocknerstrasse is the last village of any size before Heiligenblut. There used to be a second village, Bad Fusch, until it burnt down at the end of World War II.

The Grossglockner Road continues along the course of the Fuscher Ache. The mountainous section begins near the Embach Chapel after 10km. Nowhere, however, does the gradient exceed 12 percent. After the Bärenschlucht, the **Ferleiten**, a lovely mountain pasture with a wildlife park, opens up (1,145m/3,756ft). Passing the National Park Information Office you arrive at the **toll**

Above: the church at Heiligenblut.

booth ②. The charges are levied to pay for costly snow-clearing operations, maintenance of the road and environmental protection.

Passing the **Schleier Waterfall** and the Piffalpe (1,400m/4,593ft), you arrive at the Piffkar (1,620m/5,315ft). This is the starting-point for the **Piffkar panoramic footpath**. The stopping place at Hochmais affords perhaps the best view of the **Grosses**

Left: the Pasterze Glacier.

patron of mountain passes. In the middle of the tunnel you will cross the boundary to Carinthia. At the south end there is an observation point (2,500m/8,202ft) and cable car (www.skiheiligenblut.at).

In **Guttal** (1,860m/6,102ft) the road forks, and one arm extends 8km (5 miles) beside the glacier to the **Franz-Josephs-Höhe**. At the top you will find yourself facing the steep northern face of the **Grossglockner** (3,797m/ 12,467ft), the highest mountain in Austria. Looking down you have a view of the **Pasterze Glacier**, which with an area of 20 sq km (7.7 sq miles) is the largest in the eastern Alps. Apart from the visitors' centre, also here is the **Gamsgrubenweg**, a 650m (2,132ft) tunnel with an exhibition on the glacier as well as a funicular railway, the **Gletscherbahn**, leading down to the ice.

Heiligenblut

Passing the Kasereck (1,930m/6,332ft) and the Mauthaus Heiligenblut (1,700m/5,577ft), you will finally arrive in **Heiligenblut** ③ (1,300m/4,265ft), often described as the prettiest village in the Alps, with an important pilgrimage church.
SEE ALSO CHURCHES, P.61

Wiesbachhorn (3,564m/ 11,693ft), the mountain with the highest face in the eastern Alps. Just beyond is the **Haus Alpine Naturschau** (daily 9am–5pm) with an interesting exhibition on the ecology of the Hohen Tauern park.

The Hairpins

After two more bends the road crosses a landslide area of dramatically jagged rocks with the appropriate name of **Hexenküche** ('Witches' Kitchen', 2,060m/6,758ft). From the bridge on the valley side along the **Edelweisswand** (2,240m/7,349ft) you will be able to make out the remains of the so-called Roman Road; the latter is, however, a misnomer as the path was actually a trading and transport route for the gold mines dating from the Middle Ages.

At the **Fuscher Törl** (2,394m/7,854ft) there is a short side-road some 2km long leading to the **Edel-weiss-Spitze** (2,577m/ 8,455ft). It leads to the highest point along the route, from which you can enjoy a panorama of 37 mountain peaks, all more than 3,000m (9,842ft) high, and 19 glaciers.

From this point the road continues downhill, past the Fuscher Lacke (2,260m/ 7,415ft). Carry on through the 120m (394ft) long **Mittertörl Tunnel**. During excavations for the tunnel the labourers discovered a clay lamp and a statue of Hercules, the Roman

Below: the view from the Franz-Josephs-Höhe.

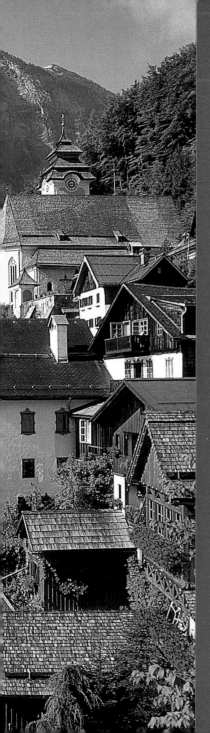

A–Z

In the following section Salzburg's and its surroundings' attractions and services are organised by theme, under alphabetical headings. Items that link to another theme are cross-referenced. All sights that lie within the atlas section at the end of the book are given a page number and grid reference.

Architecture

Architecturally, the city and surrounding region were greatly influenced by the archbishops, who during the Baroque era ruled with the might of absolute monarchs. Wolf Dietrich von Raitenau, a relative of the Medici family, became archbishop in 1587 and began to transform the little medieval town into a magnificent Baroque city along Italian lines. Entire districts of the town, then a maze of narrow, twisting alleys bordered by slender houses like those still standing in the Judengasse and Steingasse today, were demolished to make way for spacious squares with sumptuous palaces.

Early Remains

The relics of the Roman era in Salzburg (15 BC–5th century AD) include, among other things, some fine mosaic floors. The conversion of the eastern Alpine region to Christianity under St Rupert and the missionary activity centred on the Monastery of St Peter gave rise to a period of intense building activity after AD 696. By the end of the 8th century the archbishopric of Salzburg was already in possession of 67 churches and 11 monasteries.

With the development of the Romanesque style in the 11th–12th century many of the churches were remodelled. The nave of the Franciscan Church in Salzburg itself is an example of a Romanesque sacred building; other examples can be discerned only in part, due to later rebuilding, or exist only in the general overall shape. More easily recognisable are the Romanesque elements of the castles: the fortresses of Hohensalzburg and Hohenwerden were begun in 1077, Mauterndorf Castle was built

Above: a decorated ceiling in the Residenz.

in about 1250 and Moosham Castle soon afterwards.

The Gothic

The Gothic left its mark in the Chapel of St Mary in St Peter's Monastery, which was rebuilt in 1319. The Church of St Blasius, is the earliest example of a hall church (in which the nave and the aisles are of equal height) in South Germany and West Austria; built between 1327 and 1350. In 1460 came the dedication of the magnificent hall choir of the Franciscan Church, planned in 1408 by the famous architect Hans von Burghausen.

In the period between the end of the 14th and the beginning of the 16th century, churches with lofty spires were built all over the region surrounding Salzburg. St Leonard's Church at Tamsweg is a remarkable jewel of Late Gothic architecture, which not only enjoys a delightful situation but has also retained its original glass windows. In marked contrast, the most important wood carver and artist of the Late Gothic era, Michael Pacher, created works of stark realism and dynamic composition. He completed his principal work, the altar in St Wolfgang, in 1481.

The Renaissance

The Italian Renaissance reached Salzburg relatively late, The arcaded courtyard of the Spital in Salzburg (1556–62) is one of the few surviving examples of Renaissance architecture in a city in which that style was rarely seen. The marble altar (1518) in St Georgen in the Pinzgau and the frescoes of the Knights' Hall in Goldegg

Left: stucco work in the Dom.

Johann Bernhard Fischer von Erlach (1656-1723) is widely considered to have been the most influential of Austrian Baroque architects. His impact on Salzburg is widely visible in some of the city's most picturesque churches. Graz-born and trained in Rome, he devoted years to the Salzburg skyline at the end of the 17th century, leaving the distinctive mark of his later style on the Dreifaltigkeitskirche and the Kollegienkirche, as well as the Schloss Klessheim, an out of town residence for the prince-archbishops.

Castle (1536) are notable examples to be found in the surrounding region.

The Baroque

Archbishop Wolf Dietrich von Raitenau (1587–1612), began to transform the city. The construction of the Chapter House, the New Building and the Residenz in the style of magnificent palazzi began; in 1606 the archbishop also took on the court stable. Following the fire of 1598 he had the cathedral demolished completely and commissioned a new building. The new cathedral was modelled on the style of the Jesuit church, Il Gesù, in Rome.

Wolf Dietrich's successors, including Marcus Sitticus von Hohenems (1612–9) and Paris Lodron (1619–53), continued his building schemes in the Italian style; the most attractive example is Hellbrunn Palace.

The transformation of the city reached its zenith during the high and late Baroque eras, in by particular Johann Bernhard Fischer von Erlach and Johann Lukas von

Hildebrandt, who was responsible for the design of Mirabell Palace. In addition to the work of these two great masters of Austrian Baroque architecture, Salzburg also benefited from the activities of some of the country's most celebrated artists, such as Martino Altomonte, Paul Troger and Johann Michael Rottmayr.

The 19th Century

The 19th century left the Salzburg area with two interesting examples of characteristic architecture: Anif Castle, inspired by the English Gothic

style (1838–48), and the neo-Gothic Pongau Cathedral in St Johann (1855–61).

The 20th Century

The city had a lucky escape during World War II when plans drawn up for a Nazi complex inspired by Athens and built atop the Kapuzinerberg ultimately went unfulfilled. However, the century bequeathed the sensitive solution of the Festival Playhouses (1926–39 and 1956–60) by Clemens Holzmeister, and also the impressive new Museum der Moderne on the Mönchsberg.

Below: the Renaissance Civic Hospital.

Cafés and Bars

Although Salzburg cannot compete with Vienna for coffee-house culture, Salzburg's cafés are nonetheless an institution for the city. It is likely that the famous festival would not exist were it not for the Tomaselli, the Mozart, the Glockenspiel (now Demel) or the Bazar, where artists and men of letters used to meet, especially before World War II. Today the atmospheric cafés are often full to bursting point with tourists but still remain a good place to sit and watch the world go by. Belying its rather traditional outlook, Salzburg is developing a lively bar scene and some of these more trendy places are listed as well.

A stroll through the centre of Salzburg will make it clear which alcoholic drink Salzburg has adopted as its own. Stern-Bräu, Stiegl-Bräu-Keller, Augustiner-Bräustübl and other tavern signs make it only too obvious: Salzburg is a beer town, with the attractive side-effects of numerous inns and beer gardens. You can order a *grosses Bier* (½ litre) or a *kleines* (⅓ litre) from these places, which also offer a selection of good food.
SEE ALSO RESTAURANTS, P.108

The Mönchsberg

Augustiner Bräustübl
Lindhofstrasse 7; tel: 0662-431 246; www.augustinerbier.at; Mon–Fri 3–11pm, Sat–Sun 2.30–11pm; bus: 7, 20, 21, 24, 27, 28; map p.132 A4
The most popular beer garden in Salzburg, set in the brewery founded by Augustinian monks. Wonderful beer and a good choice of snacks.

M32
Museum der Moderne, Mönchsberg 32; tel: 0662-841 000; www.museumdermoderne.at; Tue–Sat 9am–1am, open Mon

Above: Demel's terrace and menus.

during Festival; map p.132 B3
The restaurant at the Museum of Modern Art also doubles as a café. The terrace overlooking the city has a stunning view and is very popular with visitors and locals alike during the summer months. They have snacks, cakes and lunches.

The Altstadt

Afro Café
Bürgerspitalplatz 5; tel: 0662-844 888; www.afrocoffee.com; Mon–Fri 10am–midnight, Sat 9am–midnight, open Sun during the Festival; map p.132 B3
A welcome alternative to the snooty delights of the likes of Tomaselli, this bright and

Left: Tomaselli, with its distinctive striped umbrellas.

newly renovated café makes a great place to sit and listen to the bells chiming in the Glockenspiel opposite. It is not as cheap as some other places but it is worth it for the location.

Dubliner
Kaigasse 8; tel: 0650 611 0967; www.dubliner.at; Mon–Fri 4pm–late, Sat–Sun 3pm–late; map p.133 C2

For anybody missing pub food, there is a wide choice of the usual fare from baked potatoes to fish and chips. Wash it all down with a pint of Guinness and, if the weather is good, there is outdoor seating too.

Fürst
Brodgasse 13, tel: 0662-843 7590; www.original-mozartkugel.com; winter: Mon–Sat 8am–8pm, Sun 9am–8pm, summer: Mon–Sat 8am–9pm, Sun 9am–9pm; map p.132 C3

A busy little café with great cakes, coffees and ice creams and a huge selection of newspapers and magazines to choose from while you relax between sightseeing expeditions. Good

colourful African-themed place is much more relaxed. Great coffee and cocktails, it is good for a rest during the day or for a drink at night. There is a good breakfast menu and in the afternoon and evening the 'African' menu kicks in with some interesting alternatives to pork and dumplings.

Café am Kai
Müllnerhauptstrasse 4; tel: 0662-420 565; www.cafe-am-kai.at; Wed–Mon 9am–8pm; bus: 7, 20, 21, 24, 27, 28; map p.132 B4

With a terrace overlooking the river, this lovely pink café is a good place to take a break when walking along the river.

Carpe Diem Finest Fingerfood
Getreidegasse 50; tel: 0662-848 800; www.carpediemfinest fingerfood.com; daily 8.30am–midnight; map p.132 C3

Both a café and a restaurant (on the first floor) on Salzburg's central street, with an attractive, modern interior. Coffee, opulent ice-creams and an excellent breakfast menu make this a

good place to head to for a spot of people-watching.

Coffee Symphony
Griesgasse 13, tel: 0699-1705 4507; www.coffee-symphony.at; Mon, Wed–Fri 9am–9pm, Sat–Sun 9.30am–9pm; map p.132 C3

Located on the first floor of this building, Sigrist has a terrace with a wonderful view of the river and the busy street below. Huge milky coffees and breakfast served until midday.

Demel
Mozartplatz 2, tel: 0662-840 358; www.demel.at; daily 9am–8pm, 9am–11pm during the Festival; map p.132 C3

The famous Viennese Café Demel took over the building that once held the Café Glockenspiel a few years ago. Now spruced up with a swish modern interior and a fabulous first floor terrace that overlooks Mozartplatz, it has become a very popular place for *Kaffee und Küche* (not least as the cakes are some of the best in town). Located on the edge of one of the busiest squares in the city, the

Austria has countless ways of preparing coffee which are named according to the size of the 'dish' in which they are served and the ratio of coffee to milk. A *kleiner Brauner* is served in a mocca cup, a *grosser Brauner* in a double mocca cup. A *Kurzer* is a strong espresso, a *Verlängerter* a weak one. *Melange* is coffee with milk and whipped cream, *Einspänner* a coffee in a tall glass with plenty of whipped cream. Many other coffee specialities include a shot of alcohol.

37

chocolate, including the infamous Mozart balls, from the shop around the corner. (Also at Mirabelleplatz 5, Sigmund Haffner Gasse and Getreidegasse 47.)

Niemetz
Herbert-von-Karajan Platz 11, tel: 662-843 367; www.sweet-niemetz.com; Mon–Sat 10am–6pm, also Sun during festival; if performances start later then the hours are extended; map p.132 B3

With an enviable location next to the Festival Halls, this café is a favourite with concert-goers and is full of festival memorabilia. You can sit over coffee, cake and a newspaper for as long as you like. The chocolate here is particularly good.

Republic
Anton-Neumayr-Platz 2; tel: 0662-841 613; www.republic-cafe.at; Sun–Thur 8am–1am, Fri–Sat 8am–4am; map p.132 B3

This café/bar/club is attched to the Republic theatre, run by Szene Salzburg. One of the liveliest places in the Altstadt (perhaps the only lively place in the Altstadt…) keep an eye on their website for the listings of club nights and DJs.

SEE ALSO FESTIVALS, P.71

Beers in Salzburg are brewed naturally in a wide range of styles and with a great deal of skill and care. **Märzen** is the equivalent to lager. (Stiegl is the local beer brewed in the city of Salzburg, Kaiser is brewed in Hallein and is the oldest brewery in Salzburg Province.) **Augustiner** is found only in the Augustinerbräu and a few other taverns. It is the monks' own special brew. It contains no gas and is quite strong. **Weissbier** is wheat beer. The yeast is not brewed out from this beer so you can see and taste it. There are three varieties: light, dark and clear. **Keller** is Zwickl and this is an unfiltered lager. **Pils** is a pale lager with a high alcohol content. **Bock** is a special occasion beer. It is only served at Christmas and Easter. It is a dark lager, which is at the top end of the alcohol content. A **Radler** is a shandy made from half lager, half lemonade.

Tomaselli
Alter Markt 9, tel: 0662-844 4880; www.tomaselli.at; daily 7am–9pm, 7am–midnight during the Festival; map p.132 C3

Dating from the early 18th century, Tomaselli's is the oldest café in Salzburg. It is

worth a visit to see the traditionally dressed waitresses wheeling trolleys full of cakes, but it is not the cheapest or friendliest café in town.

The New Town

Café Bazar
Schwarzstrasse 3; tel: 0662-874 278; www.cafe-bazar.at; Mon–Sat 7.30am–11pm, Sun 9am–6pm, 7.30am–midnight during the Festival; bus: 27; map p.132 C3

Pricey but worth it for the river views alone, both from the terrace and the salon, with its tall windows, Café Bazar has all the virtues of the classic Viennese coffee house: the latest newspapers, waiters brimming with a good-humoured and ironic superciliousness, excellent cakes, and the freedom to sit and enjoy life for as long as you can stretch a *grosser Brauner*.

Café Bellinis
Mirabellplatz 4; tel: 0662-871 385; Mon–Sat 8am–1am, Sun 11am–1am; bus: 1, 2, 3, 5, 6, 25, 840; map p.132 B4

Escape from Austro-coffee-culture into an Italianate one by stopping awhile at Bellinis. In fact, unlike any café in Italy, the swankily uni-

---

Below: cocktails in progress at the laid-back and colourful Afro Café, *see p.36*.

Above: newspapers at Sacher…

Above: …and Bellinis.

formed staff will not look at you strangely if you stay for more than five minutes and, although their cappuccino is in fact an Austrian *Melange* by any other name, it is still excellent and as enjoyable as the view of the Andräkirche across the bustling Rainerstrasse opposite. Great cocktails and a range of Italian snack foods mean that Bellinis remains an enticing venue right up to its closing time in the small hours.

Café Central

Dreifaltigkeitsgasse 3; tel: 0662-876 598; www.central-salzburg.at; Tue–Sat 9.30am–11pm; bus: 3, 5, 6, 7, 8, 20, 25, 28, 840; map p.132 C3

No relation to Freud and Trotsky's famous Viennese haunt, this café is worth keeping in mind for its comprehensive menu of breakfast options. By night it is an atmospheric meeting place, popular with locals.

Café Classic

Makartplatz 8; tel: 0662-882 700; www.cafeclassic.at; daily 7.30am–7.30pm; bus: 1, 2, 3, 5, 6, 25, 840; map p.132 C3

A bright and modern Kaffeehaus built inside Mozart's house, with smart, efficient staff, a variety of breakfast options and a good range of coffee specialities. The lunch menu offers satisfying and elegantly served bistro food.

Café Habakuk

Linzergasse 26; tel: 0662-874 150; http://www.habakuk.at; daily 9am–9pm; bus: 4; map p.132 C3

Halfway up Linzergasse, with pavement tables, the Habakuk may not offer much of a view but makes up for this with indulgent, extravagant-looking ice creams which kids will love. Try the cherry-laden Amarena Becker.

Café Primadonna

Steingasse 1; tel: 0662-870 353; www.primadonnacoffee.com; Mon–Fri 8am–8pm, Sat 9am–8pm, Sun 10am–8pm, until the 11pm during Festival; bus: 3, 5, 6, 7, 8, 20, 25, 28, 840; map p.132 C3

This most un-Austrian of venues, with coffee 'to go', nonetheless merits a visit for its successful emulation of North American café culture

(fast catching on with the locals). Good caffeine fixes for those on the move in the city centre.

Café Sacher

Schwarzstrasse 5–7; tel: 0662-88977; daily 7.30am–midnight; bus: 27; map p.132 B3

Café Sacher conjures traditional cakes alongside a healthy dose of nostalgia for the Habsburg never-never land. Like its Viennese sibling, it rather banks on the fame of the chocolate Torte which bears its name, but nonetheless the meals and cakes are good and the river view cannot be faulted.

Daimlers

Giselakai 17; tel: 0662-873 967; www.meindaimlers.at; daily 7.30pm–4am; bus: 2, 4, 21, 22; map p.133 C3

This trendy club and bar is one of the liveliest places in the New Town. It holds regular club nights (see website for details, or pick up the free listings sheet *Kultplan*) or otherwise is a good place for a drink.

Fingerlos

Franz-Josef-Strasse 9; tel: 0662-874 213; Tue–Sun

7.30am–7.30pm; bus: 21, 22; map p.132 C4

Claimed by some to serve the best coffee and cakes ever, this establishment located on the outer fringe of the Neustadt does in fact come close to deserving this hyperbolic reputation. There is a wide range of excellent, innovative and reasonably priced cakes to rival the popular riverside venues (the Champagner Torte deserves a special recommendation) and the pavement tables overlooking the Franz Josef Strasse create a pleasant sense of immersion in the daily life of the city.

Rockhouse
Schallmooser Hauptstrasse 46; tel: 0662-884 914; www.rockhouse.at; Mon–Thur 6pm–2am, Fri–Sat 6pm–4am, closed Sun unless there is live music; bus: 4; map p.133 D4

Salzburg's premier pop and rock live music venue (see website for details of coming attractions) also has one of the city's most lively bars.

The warehouse-like building – lots of industrial chic – is well worth visiting, especially when there is a band playing.

Saitensprung
Steingasse 11; tel: 0662-881 377; daily 9pm–4am; bus: 3, 5, 6, 7, 8, 20, 25, 28, 840; map p.132 C3

One of Salzburg's most popular wine and cocktail bars is tucked into the side of the Kapuzinerberg. There is a good wine list and a lively crowd, though it may be a bit of a squash to get in.

Shakespeare
Hubert-Sattler-Gasse 3; tel: 0662-879 106; www.shakespeare.at; daily 9am–2am; bus: 21, 22; map p.132 C4

As well as being an art gallery, this lively, student-oriented bar is a good place to eat, and is also a popular bar. Good cheap beer and a large list of cocktails form a major part of the attraction.

Shrimps Bar
Steingasse 5; tel: 0662-874 484; www.shrimps.at; Tue–Sun 6pm–midnight; bus: 3, 5, 6, 7, 8, 20, 25, 28, 840; map p.132 C3

Another cool place to take a cocktail or two, tiny enough to make the most standoffish patron sociable and decked out with a striking yellow interior; or tables outdoors if it all gets a bit too much for you.

Smattseer Stiftskeller
Richard Mayr Gasse 1; tel: 0662-877 2970; www.buero-salzburg.at; Mon–Sat 5pm–2am; bus: 1, 2, 3, 5, 6, 25, 840; map p.132 C3

The celler bar and pizzeria is just around the corner from the Dreifaltigkeitskirche on Mirabellplatz. As well as a good place to have a drink or a quick bit to eat there is often live music (see website for details), especially jazz.

Steinterrasse
Giselakai 3-5; tel: 0662-882 070; www.hotelstein.at; daily noon–midnight; bus: 3, 5, 6, 7, 8, 20, 25, 28, 840; map p.132 C3

Popular cocktail joint ideal for those who wish to see or be seen, especially on summer nights. Located within a stylish hotel, the views from the rooftop terrace are terrific in all directions.

Die Weisse
Rupertgasse 10; tel: 0662-872 246; www.dieweisse.at; Mon–Sat 10.30am–midnight; bus: 4; map p.133 D4

Home to a decent restaurant, the Weisse also hosts the Weissbierbrauerei, which brews a mean glass of the yeast-clouded traditional Germanic beer. The wood interior gives a friendly, pub-like air which continues into the beer garden. A perfect refuge for hot summer's afternoons.

Wirtshaus
Kapuzinerberg 9; tel: 0662-872 595; Tue–Sun 10am–sunset; map p.133 D3

A friendly bar at the summit of the Kapuzinerberg, with

Below: cakes to die for at Fingerlos.

Above: Café Bazar *(see p.38).*   **Above:** Café Classic *(see p.39).*

cool interiors and a large beer garden with excellent views. Lunch and dinner of an appropriately *Schnitzel* and *Wurst*-centred basis are available. While adults enjoy a cooling beer, children can enjoy the play equipment. The work of local artists is on display and for sale within.

Around Salzburg

Carpe Diem Lounge
Hangar-7, Wilhelm-Spazier-Strasse 7a; tel: 0662-2197; www.hangar-7.com; daily 9am–7pm; bus: 2; map p.134 C3
An elegantly furnished café, related to the more central one on Getreidegasse, housed under the glass dome of Hangar-7. Enjoy your coffee amid the ultra-modern surroundings while watching the goings-on in the museum through the glass wall.

The Salzkammergut

BAD ISCHL
Café Sissy
Pfarrgasse 2; tel: 06132-24 173; www.cafe-sissy.at; daily 8am–midnight; map p.137 D2
Given the Zauner's historical popularity with Franz Josef's mistress, it seems appropri-

ate that its principal competitor should take the name of his wife: the walls of this worthy riverside rival to Zauner Esplanade conjure the age of the Habsburgs with countless images of the empress Elisabeth, after whom the establishment is named.

Café Zauner
Pfarrgasse 7; tel: 06132-233 1020; daily 8.30am–6pm; www.zauner.at; map p.137 D2
Former bakers to the imperial court, Zauner now operate a popular and opulently decorated fin de siècle coffeehouse in true Viennese style. Pick a cake from the sumptuous selection on offer under glass before sitting down to be attended by the waiters. The rich Zaunerstollen, which recently celebrated its centenary, is particularly renowned. On the riverfront, Zauner run a sister venue with attractive views: Zauner Esplanade (daily 10am–10pm).

Giovanni's
Kreuzplatz 4; tel: 06132-23 976; www.eis-giovanni.at; daily from 8.30am; map p.137 D2
Ice cream parlour with sibling cafés in Bad Aussee, Ebensee and Hallstatt, Giovanni's is always a good

place for working off all those good intentions and spa sessions with an indulgent gelato sundae. Venues large and small are scattered all around Bad Ischl (including Schröpferplatz), but Kreuzplatz is the main *Eissalon.*

ST GILGEN
Café Nannerl
Kirchenplatz 2; tel: 06227-2368; www.cafenannerl.at; summer daily 11am–11pm; map p.135 E3
The relaxed and friendly Café Nannerl is right in the centre of town. It is named after Mozart's talented sister; the composer's mother was also born in this small town making some sense of the connection. The café offers a traditional range of cakes, coffee and other drinks amid a charming imperial-nostalgic décor.

Salzburg is not exactly noted for its gay and lesbian nightlife. In general there is little overt discrimination and the city is very safe. The local gay and lesbian organisation HOSI (Gabelsbergerstrasse 26; tel: 0662-4359 2727; www.hosi.or.at) holds occasional nights at places like argekultur *(see Literature and Theatre, p.93).* Bars that are gay- and lesbian-friendly include Daimlers *(see p.39),* and the city has three friendly and welcoming specifically gay venues, all of which are in the New Town: **Mexx** (Schallmooser Hauptstrasse 20; www.mexxgaybar.at; Sun–Thur 8.30pm–4am, Fri–Sat 8.30pm–5am); **Birdy's** (Schallmooser Hauptstrasse 25; www.birdys.at; daily 5pm–4am) and the **Zwei Stein** (Giselakai 9; tel: 662-877 179; www.zweistein.at; daily 6pm–4am).

Castles and Palaces

Salzburg's history as a strategically important trade route and source of valuable salt have combined with its wealth and the devotion to architecture of its princes to leave an impressive legacy of castle and palace-building. Grand edifices range from the Baroque delights of the city's own Schloss Mirabell, with its floral gardens stretching to the waterfront and a semi-salacious history as the home to an archbishop's consort, to the ruined but once strategically vital Schloss Wildenstein overlooking Bad Ischl.

The charm of Salzburg's fortresses and their conversion to leisure purposes by the tourist industry today, not only in the city but also across the province and the wider Salzkammergut, hide the pragmatic strategic needs that brought about

Below: the State Rooms' Gothic percelain stove.

their construction. For example, the Rudolfsturm at Hallstatt's salt mines is little more than an echo of Salzburg's medieval past, but in 1284 it was a vital element in the defence of Habsburg regional interests and its Gothic charms in fact testify to the intense militarisation of this province over many centuries. The variety of edifices within the region is impressive and is a major attraction for travellers.

Mönchsberg

Festung Hohensalzburg

Mönchsberg 34; tel: 0662-8424 3011; Fortress: www.salzburg-burgen.at, Fortress Museum: www.salzburgmuseum.at, Ranier-Regimentsmuseum: www.rainer-regimentsmuseum-salzburg.at, FestungsBahn: www.salzburg-ag.at; daily Oct–Apr: 9.30am–5pm, May–Sept: 9am–7pm; entrance charge covers all sites; map p.132 C2

The Hohensalzburg Fortress dominates the city's countenance like a crown of stone. Even if you have no time for an official conducted tour,

you should still find time to stand on the vast Kuenburg Bastion and gaze down on the streets and houses. The fortress itself is well worth a few hours' attention if you have the time, as it is one of the largest and best-preserved castles in Europe.

You can take the funicular up to the fortress at the end of the Festungsgasse (the Festungsbahn). Alternatively, if you are feeling more energetic you can make your way up on foot (there is a staircase near the valley station). This will give you an opportunity to appreciate the precipitous nature of the rock and the impregnability of the complex.

HISTORY

The Hohensalzburg has had a fascinating history under its many ruling archbishops. Construction began in 1077 under the reign of Archbishop Gebhard and it was constantly enlarged and renovated up until the 17th century. The Late Gothic appearance of the fortress is largely due to the building work of the 15th-century

Left: the Festung Hohen-salzburg in the evening light.

The **State Rooms** in the Hohen Stock can be visited as part of a the **Fortress Museum**. The princely apartments and banqueting halls on the upper floor are some of the most beautiful Late Gothic secular interiors in the whole of Europe. Of particular interest are the Golden Hall, with magnificent wood panelling and carvings, and the Golden Room, in which stands a brightly-coloured porcelain tiled stove (1501).

The exhibits in the museum (daily: winter 9.30am–5pm, summer 9am–7pm) itself refer to the fortress's history and include musical instruments, armour and models of the fortress at various points in its history. The arefacts in the museum have recently been redisplayed to great effect.

THE INNER ROOMS AND OTHER MUSEUMS

A conducted tour of the fortress battlements leaves from the entrance at the bottom of the Hasen Bastion (Hare Tower). The audio guide that accompanies explains the portraits you see and the rooms, including the dungeon, that you pass through. The literal highlight

Above: musical instruments on display in the Fortress Museum.

archbishop Leonhard von Keutschach (1495–1519), who was not only a religious leader but also, like many of the archbishops, a powerful temporal ruler. He therefore needed constant protection from outside invasion and even revolts from within his own territories. It was during this period that the main building of the fortress was significantly enlarged. There is a marble memorial to von

Keutschach on the wall of St George's Church, and he is also commemorated by numerous insignia and coats of arms that all include his curious personal symbol, identified by some as a turnip, by others as a beet-root. Since the days of von Keutschach, the lion that is the symbol of the fortress has held a turnip (or beet-root) in its paws.

The Hohensalzburg was more than just a defensive fortress and residence in war-torn times. During periods when there was no direct military threat to the city, it was used as a barracks and a prison. Archbishop Wolf Dietrich von Raitenau was held prisoner there by his nephew and successor, Markus Sittikus, for five years until his death in 1617.

THE COURTYARD AND MUSEUM

In the outer fortress courtyard stands a lime tree, which is several hundred years old, and the Fortress Well (1539). Also here is the Church of St George (1501–2).

One curious exhibit that can be seen on the tour of the fortress's inner rooms is the Salzburg Bull, one of the earliest remaining street organs (1502). The horn mechanism was linked to a barrel mechanism in the middle of the 16th century. Renovation work began in 2000 and the organ now roars in reply to the Glockenspiel once again.

Above: gilded decoration in the Mirabell Palace.

of the tour is observation tower where the views over the city and surrounding mountains is superb.

Also in the Hohen Stock at the centre of the castle is the **Rainer-Regimentsmuseum** (daily: summer 9am–7pm, winter 9.30am–5pm) which recalls the Imperial and Royal Regiment of Archduke Rainer; most poignant are the displays from the terrible Alpine battles of World War I.

The interesting **Marionette Museum** (daily: summer 9am–7pm, winter 9.30am–5pm), in the cellars of the fortress, displays historical puppets from the Salzburg Marionette Theatre and is always a hit with children.

The Altstadt

Residenz State Rooms
Residenzplatz; tel: 0662-8404

> Salzburg's Schloss Fürberg narrowly escaped a disastrous end when on 3rd September 1955, a plane crashed into the Kapuzinerberg near the palace, tragically costing the lives of the pilot and three passengers.

510; www.salzburg-burgen.at; daily 10am–5pm; entrance charge; map p.132 C3

The west side of the Residenzplatz is occupied by the Residenz. Its origins stretch back as far as 1110, when the archbishop, who no longer held the office of Abbot of St Peter's, built himself the first Bishop's Palace. The Residenz's present-day appearance is the result of extensions and rebuilding begun by Archbishop Wolf Dietrich von Raitenau before 1600, but not completed until the late 18th century. The complex encloses three courtyards. The marble entrance on the Residenzplatz leads into the main courtyard. Passing through the triple-arched portico with a Fountain of Hercules, take the staircase on the left which leads up to the sumptuous reception rooms. The decorations adorning the audience rooms and the private apartments of the archbishops are by a succession of famous artists, including Johann Michael Rottmayr, Martino Altomonte, Johann

Lukas von Hildebrandt and Antonio Beduzzi.

Schloss Leopoldskron
Leopoldskronstrasse 56–8; tel: 0662-839 830; www.schloss-leopoldskron.com; map p.132 B1

A short walk south from the Nonntal area of the Old Town takes you to the Leopoldskron district, which contains the lake and palace of the same name. The Leopoldskron Palace was built by Archbishop Firmian in 1736 in rococo style.

The archbishops used the palace for centuries, but in the early 20th century, it was bought by Max Reinhardt, one of the founders of the Salzburg Festival. He had it totally renovated and had the gardens laid out in their present form.

Now the property of an American institute, it is used for conferences and seminars but unfortunately is not open to the public. However, you can see the palace from the lakeside path, which provides a lovely walk at any time of year. In the summer, the swans are wonderful to watch and in winter, the Salzburgers love to use the lake for ice-skating and curling matches.

The New Town

Schloss Arenberg
Arenbergstrasse 10; tel: 0662-640 1010; www.aaf-online.org; map p.133 D3

This palace atop the Bürgelstein has a long history beginning with the Roman occupation of what was then Celtic Noreaia around 15 BC. The 'Arenbergstrasse' over which the Roman camp watched was an important strategic route between the Alps and the Adriatic. From the end of the 17th century, the castle was in the possession of the prince archbishops of Salzburg.

Above: the golden façade of Schloss Hellbrunn.

A later owner, Sebastian Rosenegger, purchased the site and produced an exemplary landscape garden in the terraced, English style which attracted visitors from across the continent. His son and heir Josef would later earn notoriety by augmenting the sale of Roman artefacts found on the site with fakes in order to increase the estate's income.

The palace was severely damaged by fire in the early years of the 19th century and was renovated in the then-fashionable Biedermeier style: these features remain intact today. The palace served as residence to a number of artists and an academic institute before it was purchased in 2001 by the American Austrian Foundation. It now serves as an international conference centre as well as a base for the Vienna Philharmonic Orchestra when it moves from the capital to Salzburg province for the Festspiele season. In 2009 the Schloss again suffered considerable fire damage but has been completely rebuilt and is again functioning as a conference centre.

Schloss Mirabell
Mirabellplatz 4; tel: 0662-8072; www.stadt-salzburg.at; map p.132 B4

This early 17th-century palace was built by Archbishop Wolf Dietrich for his mistress Salome Alt. The number of their illegitimate children ran to double figures. Dietrich's successor, Marcus Sitticus, appropriated Alt's palace as an additional residence, renaming it from 'Altenau' to remove the allusion to his predecessor's infidelities. While it is now used by the city administration to house the mayor's office and various other departments, during working hours it is still possible to enter the reception, its marble staircase adorned with Baroque sculptures by Georg Raphael Donner (daily 8am–6pm; free). The equally ornate Marble Hall (Mon, Wed–Thur 8am–4pm, Tue, Fri 1–4pm; free), to which the staircase leads, plays host to lunchtime and evening concerts (www.salzburger-schlosskonzerte.at). The palace's **gardens** are, however, open to the public (daily 6am–sunset) and are the most popular formal park in the city.

Schloss Neuhaus
Kühbergstrasse 1

Despite being known as the 'New House', this palace complex is in fact centuries old, with experts struggling to give an exact date to its foundation, although it certainly existed at the beginning of the 13th century. After centuries in service to the Salzburg archbishops and the local government, it has been in private hands since 1963. The Schloss is currently owned by a German industrialist Hubertus Benteler who plans to use it as his headquarters.

Around Salzburg
Schloss Aigen
Schwarzenbergpromenade 37

This modest palace, currently owned by the Revert-era family, was first built in 1402 and underwent many transformations over the years, especially under the ownership of the Schwarzenbergs who developed the gardens. While the name 'Schloss Aigen' has been adopted by a neighbouring restaurant, the palace's main attractions today are the

45

The palace's main attractions are the **Surprise Fountains** in the garden. The bishop had the idea of having them built following a lengthy stay in Rome; here, however, he carried the surprise element to extremes. Unexpectedly, water fountains would suddenly gush forth from the stone seats and soak the guests sitting at the table in the Roman theatre; unexpected, that is, except for the bishop himself, who was vastly amused at the joke.

Visitors should also be prepared for surprises in the various grottoes, which are arranged according to mythological themes. Nowadays the guides are equally unconcerned about water damage to the expensive cameras carried by visitors, so beware. Hydraulic power is also used to drive a number of smaller machines and a large mechanical theatre with an organ which runs on water power.

Many of Salzburgs castles and palaces festure in *The Sound of Music*. Much of the film was made on location in and around the city and today, scores of fans still flock to retrace the Trapp family's steps. Anif Castle *(above)* features in the opening shots and among the locations used in the film were the Mirabell Gardens where 'Do Re Mi' was sung around the fountain. St Peter's Cemetery was reconstructed in the studios and used for the scene where the Trapp family hide between the tombstones when trying to escape detection by the Nazis. The facade of Fohnburg Castle was used as the front of the Trapp villa while Leoploldskron Castle was used as the rear of the villa. The children go boating on the lake there and the ballroom was modelled on one of the rooms inside. The opening scenes in the convent were filmed at Nonnberg Abbey; the famous opening credit scenes were filmed around Lake Fuschl and the wedding at the church in Mondsee. The von Trapp family make their escape over the Untersberg and many other places are used in the film.

waterfalls which adorn the gardens, now opened to the public as a nature park enjoyed by many local residents. The suburb of Salzburg to which it lends its name was home to the real Von Trapp family.

Schloss Hellbrunn

Fürstenweg 37; tel: 0662-8203 720; www.hellbrunn.at; daily Apr and Oct–Nov: 9am–4.30pm, May–June and Sept: 9am–5.30pm, July–Aug: 9am–9pm; entrance charge; bus: 25; map p.134 C3

The layout and design of this palace built for Markus Sittikus follow the lines of a typical Italian *villa suburbana*. It was probably built in 1613–5 under the supervision of the architect in charge of the reconstruction of the cathedral, Santino Solari. The interior is no longer complete, but the frescoes in the banqueting hall and the adjoining music room in the octagonal pavilion still provide first-class examples of the Mannerist style: with views of a city in the background, the *trompe-l'oeil* painting shows imaginary scenes of buildings with aristocrats strolling among them.

Schloss Klessheim

Schloss Klessheim, Wals; tel: 0662-8544 550; www.casinos.at; daily noon–3am; bus: 18; map p.134 C3

The main part of Klessheim Palace, about 1.5km (1 mile) west of the city centre, was built by Johann Fischer von Erlach for Archbishop Johann Ernst Thun between 1700 and 1709. He used designs and ideas from the Versailles palace and gardens and eventually completed the construction in 1732. It was used by the archbishops until Salzburg came under the control of the Habsburgs. In

Right: Mauterndorf Castle.

the late 19th century, Emperor Franz Josef banished his homosexual younger brother, Archduke Ludwig Viktor, to Klessheim Palace after Ludwig had sparked a public scandal by making advances to an army officer in a swimming pool in Vienna. He died here in 1919.

Between 1938 and 1945, Hitler used the palace as his residence when he was in Salzburg. It was here that he met the Italian dictator Mussolini in 1940 and other heads of state from Hungary, Czechoslovakia and Romania. After the war, it became the headquarters of the occupying army. Then for a long time it was used by the provincial government to receive state visitors. Since 1993, it has housed the city's casino. The gardens and a few rooms of the palace can be seen for free, but there is a fee to get into the casino.

The Salzkammergut

Kaiservilla
Jainzen 38, Bad Ischl; tel: 06132-232 41; www.kaiservilla.com; continuous tours: daily May–Sept 9.30am–5pm, Oct 10am–4pm; hourly tours: Dec, Sat–Sun 10am–4pm, Jan–Mar, Wed 10am–4pm, Apr, daily 10am–4pm; entrance charge; map p.137 D2

An imperial summer retreat for well over half a century, the Kaiservilla at Bad Ischl is another must-see for anyone with an interest in the time of the Habsburgs. An engagement present for Franz Josef

and his Bavarian fiancée, the villa would later play host to the emperor's mistress, the actress and singer Katharina Schratt. She would, with the empress' approval, discreetly move between the imperial residence and her own villa, linked by a nearby footpath. When not otherwise engaged with his mistress or the burdens of government, Franz Josef would dispense with a frankly terrifying number of animals, shooting some tens of thousands of chamois and other woodland creatures over more than 60 years' worth of holiday residence. Guided tours of the premises include Habsburg family

Wildenstein Ruins
On the outskirts of Bad Ischl lies all that remains of the only major castle within the inner Salzkammergut region. A clearly marked and undemanding trail of 4½km leads uphill from the Esplanade to the castle walls and an excellent vantage point over the town itself.

busts and portaiture, countless hunting mementoes and trophies, and the study from which Franz Josef would exercise his powers as head of state. It was here that he put his name to a declaration of war, following the death of Archduke Franz Ferdinand, which brought about World War I and the ultimate breakup of the Habsburg Empire.

The Marmorschlössl behind the villa, a marble folly in the villa garden, houses a collection of exhibits on the camera, but it was originally constructed for the Empress Elisabeth to retire to while her husband indulged himself at the Kaiservilla.

SEE ALSO MUSEUMS AND GALLERIES, P.102

Schloss Scharnstein
Almtal, Gmunden; tel: 0664-300 5677; www.kriminalmuseum.at; May–Oct, Tue–Thur, Sat–Sun 9am–5pm; entrance charge; map p.137 E3

A little further out of Gmunden you will find Schloss Scharnstein. The castle dates back to the second half of the 16th century, and today has been converted to house a range of

rather dark but utterly fascinating visitor attractions.

These include a collection of reptiles and insects, and a museum of policing which tends to the graphic in its accounts of both murderers' misdeeds and punishments historically meted out by the authorities. There is also a museum of Austrian history since the fall of empire, which holds fascinating display materials, but is as mealy-mouthed on Austrian culpability in mid- to late-20th-century persecution and oppression as the museum at Ebensee is clear-eyed and critical.

SEE ALSO MUSEUMS AND GALLERIES, P.103

Schloss Weyer
Karl-Josef-von-Frey-Gasse 27, Gmunden; tel: 07612-65018; Jun–Sept: Tue–Fri 10am–noon, 2–5.30pm; entrance charge; map p.137 E3

Close to the Seeschloss Ort on Gmunden's Freygasse is the Renaissance-built Schloss Weyer. It is privately owned but puts on temporary exhibitions, the most recent was on Meissner porcelain from Dresden.

Seeschloss Ort
Orth 1, Gmunden; tel: 07612-624 99; www.schlossorth.com; map p.137 E3

This 15th-century castle at Gmunden is most famous for playing host to a television series, *Schlosshotel Orth*, which gathered a devoted fan audience over nine years and 113 episodes. The show followed the highs and lows of life, love and intrigue among its guests and staff. Against the tranquil background of the lake, events worthy of any American daytime soap took place; the hotel's first director died of a heart attack after rescuing a child from drowning, while another member of staff was killed off in an early episode only for the same actress to return in a new role half-way through the series. The castle is now used as a restaurant and a conference centre.

Left: Schloss Moosham.

Left: Hohenwerfen.

trade route. Frequent additions up to the 16th century have given it a fairytale appearance. It was used as a prison for many centuries and among those locked up there was Archbishop Wolf Dietrich von Raitenau in 1611. The castle museum has an armoury, and there are daily falconry displays (mid-Jul–Aug Apr–mid-Jul 11am, 2.15 and 4.30pm, Sept–Oct 11am and 3pm). If the castle seems familiar to you, it may be because it was used in the 1968 film *Where Eagles Dare*.

Schloss Goldegg
Hofmark 1, Goldegg; tel: 06415-8123; www.museum-goldegg.at; Mon–Tue, Thur–Sat 10am–noon, 3–5pm, Sun 3–5pm, guided tour daily 2pm; entrance charge; map p.138 C3
This *Schloss* can trace its origins back to a building dating from 1323; over the years it underwent reconstruction on a number of occasions and has recently been meticulously restored. The Knights' Hall has wood panelling dating from about 1500 and frescoes from 1536, which make it the most important example of interior decoration dating purely from this era in the Salzburg region. Today, the castle is a conference and exhibition centre and also houses the Pongau Regional Museum.

The Lammertal and Lungau

Burgerlebnis Mauterndorf
5570 Mauterndorf; tel: 06472-7426; www.salzburg-burgen.at; daily May–Oct: 10am–6pm, Tue, Thur Jan–Mar: 11am–6pm; entrance charge; map p.139 D3
Looking at first glance like a giant toy, the castle at Mauterndorf was built by the Cathedral Chapter of Salzburg in 1253 to protect the valley and the village. Today the castle is a cultural centre and houses the Lungau Regional Museum, which has an interesting array of exhibits. The castle chapel dates from 1339 and boasts the oldest Gothic frescoes in the Salzburg region (1350), as well as a winged altar dating from 1452. The castle's restaurant (www.burg schaenke.at) provides an atmospheric place for a meal.

Schloss Moosham
Moosham 12, Unternberg; tel: 06476-305; www.schloss-moosham.info; daily Apr–Oct: 9am–4pm; entrance charge; map p.139 D2
This fortification was first mentioned in records in 1256. Originally a courthouse, its main business was concerned with the prosecution of men and women suspected of being witches and wizards; it possesses a torture chamber as well as rooms with period furnishings. Today there is also a castle tavern where visitors can find refreshment during their visit.

The Salzach and High Tauern

Erlebnisburg Hohenwerfen
Werfen; tel: 06468-7603; www.salzburg-burgen.at; daily May–June and Sept: 9am–5pm, July–Aug: 9am–6pm, Oct: 9.30am–4pm, Apr: Tue–Sun 9.30–4pm; entrance charge; map p.136 C1
Castle Hohenwerfen was built in 1077 to guard the

> According to folklore, the dungeons in Werfen were sometimes filled to capacity with innocent people, including Protestant missionaries who had offended the archbishops of Salzburg in some way. It is said that these 'unwanted sorts' were locked up in darkness in solitary confinement for years and only set free after they had gone mad.

Caves and Mines

The geology of the Salzburg region not only provided its wealth but has given rise to some of its most impressive features. The limestone High Alps rise vertically from the valleys and their high rainfall and melting ice and snow have scoured vertical karst chimneys and caves in the limestone mountains. The gorges of the Saalach Valley bear impressive witness to the power of water as do the underground river passages and caverns. In the Eisriesenwelt caves in the Tennengebirge and in the Dachstein Caves, the cold air in winter has frozen the seeping water into unusual shapes.

Dachstein Ice Caves

Obertraun; tel: 01631-5310; www.dachsteinwelterbe.at; daily, Jun–Aug: first tour 9.20am last tour 4.30pm, Sept–Oct, May first tour 9.20am last tour 4pm; entrance charge, includes cable car; map p.137 D1

Among the most famous attractions of the Salzkammergut, the caves at Dachstein are reached from the village of Obertraun, accessible from Hallstatt by boat, bus, or 3-minute train ride. For the caves and village, stop at Obertraun-Dachsteinhöhlen; the other Obertraun stop is only for the water caves. Although the caverns are millions of years old, the ice within has barely reached its fifth centenary and continues to grow year by year. The caves are clearly signposted from the Dachstein cable car's first stop, which also houses their ticket office. The Giant Ice Caves form the principal attraction, seen on an hour-long tour which departs every half-hour. The lesser Mammoth Caves, with their 'Midnight Cathedal' located

Above: taking the *Seilbahn* to Eisreisenwelt.

at their ultimate extremity, are festooned with additional *son et lumière* to boost their relative attraction; despite the artifice, the effect is very powerful, as a well-judged combination of music and projected abstract imagery complements the natural ambience of the caverns.

Eisriesenwelt

Werfen; tel: 06468-5248; www.eisriesenwelt.at; daily May–Oct: first tour 9am last tour 3.30pm, July–Aug: first tour 9am last tour 4.30pm; entrance charge, includes cable car; map p.136 C1

The caves of Eisriesenwelt ('World of the Ice Giants'), east of Werfen, are the largest ice caves in Europe. First explored in 1879, they stretch for about 42km (26 miles), although only a fraction of that length is open to the public. Fantastic ice 'statues' and frozen waterfalls extend for about 1km (0.5 mile) from the entrance. The ice formations are created during the winter months when the water in the caves freezes, so the best time to see them is in the spring and early summer before the formations have started to melt again. Take the bus from Werfen's main square, then it is a 15-minute walk from the car park/bus stop to the cable car station. The *Seilbahn* takes you from 1,084 to 1,586m (3,556 to 5,203ft) and the view is stupendous. In order to enter the

Left: the 'Ice Cathedral' in the Dachstein caves.

tour 4.30pm, Sept: first tour 9.30am last tour 3.30pm, Oct: first tour 9.30am last tour 3pm; entrance charge; map p.137 D1

7,000 years old and still going strong, Hallstatt's salt mines are the oldest in the world. Established by the Celtic culture to which the town lends its name, the Salzbergwerk formed the basis for prosperity in the region across millennia, and if tourism is as important as excavation in today's mines, this only reflects the changed priorities of contemporary Austria. The Rudolfsturm, a fortified tower which once guarded the mines from the European rivals between which Salzburg lay wedged, now serves coffees and a famed *Gugelhupf*, the marbled cake favoured by Freud. The caverns once worked industriously under the prince-archbishops of the province, but now play host to visitors on an elaborate tour by underground railway and chute through wondrous caverns, including one housing an entire lake. Even the ascent to the site can become

The water caves, or **Koppen-brüllerhöhle**, in Dachstein (www.dachsteinwelterbe.at; daily May–Sept: first tour 9am last tour 4pm; entrance charge), are semi-submerged caverns hosting a giant natural spring. Although they are served by their own train stop in the summer season, they are only a short walk from the village proper.

the names for the ice formations created when the melting snow froze: the Hymir Hall, Frigga's Veil and Odin's Room. There is a vast ice cathedral named after the explorer of the caves, Alexander von Mork (1887–1914), who was also buried here.

Hallstatt Salzbergwerk
Salzbergstrasse 21, 4830 Hallstatt; tel: 06132-200 2400; www.salzwelten.at; daily, Apr–Aug: first tour 9.30am last

caves, you have to take one of the many guided tours that start at regular intervals. As the temperature inside is always around freezing point, you will need warm clothing and sensible shoes to negotiate the narrow slippery passages. The caves are not recommended for the elderly, infirm or children. Although it is quite a strenuous excursion, it is certainly worth the effort. Once inside the caves you enter a fairy-tale world in which figures from Nordic and German mythology provide

Right: looking up at the Eisreisenwelt caves and the spectacular view from the top.

Left: the miners' slide in the Hallein salt mines.

tors, and the breathtaking enclosed salt lake at the heart of the tour.

HALLSTÄTTER GRÄBERFELD

The modern Salzbergwerk is intimately connected with the history of the Celtic culture that first mined the area. In 1846, it was a mine director, Johann Georg Ramsauer, who identified a Celtic graveyard which he began to explore. In less than 20 years he had uncovered and documented 980 graves, the pioneering work of archaeology in what would turn out to be the resting place of more than 4,000 people and one of the world's most significant burial finds from antiquity. Much of what Ramsauer uncovered now lies in Vienna's Naturhistorisches Museum, but Hallstatt is still recognised as a key location in the cultural history of antiquity.

Salzbergwerk Altaussee

Lichtersberg 25, 8992 Altaussee; tel: 06132-200 2400; www.salzwelten.at; daily, May, mid-Sept–Oct: tours at 9 and 11am, 1 and 3pm, Jun–mid-Sept: hourly tours 9am–4pm, Nov–Dec: Wed 7pm, Jan–Apr: Wed 5 and 7pm; entrance charge; map p.137 E1

A significant salt mining facility in the Salzkammergut lies

> The Nazis did not just exploit the Salzkammergut's caves to hide their thefts. The caves of the Seeberg were excavated as bomb-proof industrial areas using forced labour from the Ebensee concentration camp. A memorial to the camp inmates stands in the caverns today. *(See also Monuments, p.97).*

> Gastein Valley Entrische Kirche is one of the largest stalagmite caves in the Central Alps; during the Counter-Reformation it was used by Protestants as a secret place of worship. From Klammstein a footpath with a nature trail leads to the cave entrance (45 minutes; tours May–Jun: Wed–Mon 11am, noon, 2 and 3pm, Jul–Aug: daily 11am, noon, 2, 3 and 4pm, Sept: Wed–Mon noon and 2pm; entrance charge).

close to the town of Bad Aussee. It has been open to visitors for more than 100 years, although today it is more widely accessible than when the likes of scientist Alexander von Humboldt or the Habsburg Archduke Johann received their VIP tours. The 800-year-old site, which today also includes a quarry, is the largest of its kind in Austria, producing 400,000 tonnes of salt a year. It even has its own chapel, built out of salt blocks and dedicated to St Barbara. It offers English-language tours of both the working galleries and the historical curios, as well as other wonders including an underground lake.

HIDDEN ART

The Altaussee fulfilled a more infamous role in World War II in what Austrians refer to as *Kunstschätzen*, or 'art protecting'; it was the bomber-proof hiding place of many thousands of artworks purloined under the Nazi regime. The *Springerwerk*, which was chosen in 1943 as the hiding place for these pieces, is today open to the public. It is preserved as it was in the Nazi era, giving silent testi-

an adventure by riding the **Salzbergbahn** funicular railway which ascends from the town to the facility itself. The Salzbergwerk's tours today concentrate on the figure of the *Mann im Salz*, or 'Man in Salt', a Celtic miner whose body was found by workers, perfectly preserved in salt, in 1734. The mines' official diary entry for the day describes the discovery of a corpse, 'flat as a board and gone hard as stone', preserved complete with intact tools and clothing. The tour combines a dramatic illustration of the physical and contemporary aspects of mining with an account of prehistoric Hallstatt culture and society. The life and times of the *Mann im Salz* provides a welcome human focus to the awe-inspiring sights on the tour, with local actor Gerhard Schilcher bringing the figure to life on-site in an additional attraction for German-speakers. As a bonus, children will love the system of slides and underground railways used to transport visi-

Right: a tunnel in the Hallein salt mine.

mony to wartime misdeeds. The shelves once held the most famous works of Europe's artists, including those of Michelangelo, Van Dyck, Dürer, Rubens and Vermeer. In 1945, with the war evidently lost, the Nazi commander in Linz decided to destroy the mines and the artworks along with them. Eight bombs were smuggled into the cavern with signs marking them as marble items, to be handled with care. Local mountain workers discovered the deception and removed them from the Salzbergwerk.

Salzbergwerk Berchtesgaden

Bergwerkstrasse 83, 83471 Berchtesgaden; tel: 00 49 8652-600 20; www.salzzeitreise.de; daily, May–Oct: first tour 9am last tour 5pm, Nov–Apr: first tour 11am last tour 3pm; entrance charge; map p.134 C1

Salt has been mined in Berchtesgaden since 1517, and still is today. Visitors are issued with old miners' cloth-ing for a tour of the mines, accompanied by a miner, starting in a small truck on railway tracks. The rest of the tour includes sliding down a miners' chute into the enormous 'Salt Cathedral' and taking a ferry across an underground salt lake.

Salzbergwerk Hallein/ Bad Dürrnberg

Raumsustrasse 3, 5422 Bad Dürrnberg; tel: 06132-200 8511; www.salzwelten.at; daily, Feb–Mar, Nov–Dec: first tour 10am last tour 3pm, Apr–Oct: first tour 9am last tour 5pm; entrance charge; map p.135 C1

Salt was once mined on the Dürrnberg (770m/2,526ft). Today, the excavations are focussed on the Celtic settlements which once stood here; successfully, too, as the Dürrnberg is one of the largest Celtic archaeological sites. There is evidence that the Dürrnberg was settled as long ago as Neolithic times (around 2000 BC). Settlements grew up here during the late Hallstatt era and the La Tène era (from 600 BC). Around 200 BC, mining stopped and the inhabitants moved away. At the end of the 12th century, salt production started up again and became one of the important sources of income of the prince-bishops of Salzburg. In 1989 the mine (which had produced 40,000 tonnes of salt annually) closed because it was no longer economically viable. Now the mines are closed and have been turned into a museum. A tour of the Dürrnberg Salt Mines, conducted by 'Prince Archbishop Wolf Dietrich von Raitenau' and his side-kick Jakobus, demonstrates how salt was mined, explains the importance of salt and gives visitors the chance to go on an underground boat trip and a slide down an old miners' chute. Also included in the entrance charge is the Celtic Village, a reconstruction of a village showing how the Celts lived and worked.

Children

Despite a reputation for stern upbringing – think of Captain von Trapp and that whistle – Austrians are a people very much fond of children, so younger travellers and their carers should not have any difficulty with accommodation, dining or visiting attractions. That said, Austrian children are well-mannered and people will not expect to make much concession for noise or misbehaviour in restaurants or other facilities. However, the Austrian tradition of *Gastfreundlichkeit* means that staff will largely do their very best to facilitate the travels of those with young children.

Hallstatt

Children will love the system of slides and underground railways used to transport visitors, and the breathtaking enclosed salt lake at the heart of the tour of the salt mines. The town's museum also caters well for younger travellers, with a simulated avalanche experience (possibly too frightening for the very young) and even an exhibit devoted to prehistoric poo.
SEE ALSO CAVES AND MINES, P.51; MUSEUMS AND GALLERIES, P.103

The Marionette Theatre

An attraction that is of particular interest to families is the city's puppet theatre. Although taking the kids to the opera may not be the first

> Although menus specifically designed for children are particularly thin on the ground, most chefs are willing to adapt some basic dish (often pasta) to suit the demands of even the most particular young diners; and you might find that dedicated changing facilities or hotel day care are rarer still.

Above: puppets line up in preparation for a production of *The Marriage of Figaro* at the Marionette Theatre.

thought that passes through the average family traveller's mind, the shows here are a genuine delight, offering a captivating and magical spectacle suitable for children of all ages.
SEE ALSO LITERATURE AND THEATRE, P.93

The Mirabellgarten

The Zauberflötchen Playground, named for Mozart's opera, is a bright, exquisite modern play area in a quiet corner of Salzburg's Mirabell Garden. It includes an enormous climbing frame with slide, interconnected swings and much more besides. A

fabulous place for young hearts to burn off some of that *Strudel*.

Mozarteis

Mozartplatz; tel: 0662-881 0120; www.mozarteis.at; Nov–Jan: Mon–Fri 12.30–2pm, 2.30–6.30pm, 5–7pm, 7.30–9.30pm, Sat–Sun also 10am–noon; entrance charge; map p.133 C3
The annual outdoor skating rink on Mozartplatz is great fun for adults and children alike. It is a lovely place to have a quick spin around the ice, and there are also stalls where the grown-ups can indulge in a *Glühwein*.

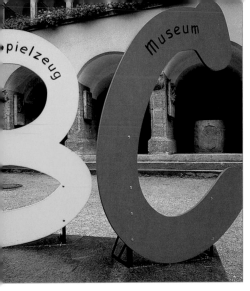

multimedia environment; perfect for calming down after an energetic day's splashing. Bad Ischl's Kaisertherme has no facilities specifically aimed at children, but the spa pools with their water jets are nonetheless good for an hour or two's fun.
SEE ALSO SPAS, P.118–9

Zoo Salzburg

Anifer Landesstrasse 1, 5081 Anif; tel: 0662-820 176; www.salzburg-zoo.at; daily, Nov–Mar: 9am–4pm, Mar–Jun, Sept–Oct 9am–5pm, Jul–Aug 9am–6.30pm; entrance charge; map p.135 C3

Less depressing and prison-like than some places, this zoo has a large collection of birds and mammals that will delight children. Highlights include the large cats and the Alpine animals. The use of semi-open pens means that visitors can get close to the inhabitants. Some of the birds, such as the vultures or flamingos can be seen either around the peak of the Untersberg, or in Leopold-skron farm ponds. Feeding times are especially interesting and, in the summer, the zoo is open at night (July–Aug, Fri and Sat until 11pm).

Below: the Krampus runs riot in Salzburg.

A Christmas visit to Salzburg may involve running a gauntlet of monsters. In local tradition, Father Christmas is assisted by the Krampus, a hairy demonic creature responsible for punishing naughty children undeserving of presents. Locals dressed as the Krampus may sometimes pounce on the unwary during the carnival-esque Christmas markets.

The Open Air Museum

Grossgmain's **Freilichtmu-seum** is a great spot for kids, especially in fine weather. The site has reconstructions of rural and agricultural life in the province from the 16th to 20th centuries. Demonstra-tions of traditional arts and crafts usually take place at the weekends, while school holidays offer a range of weekday workshops aimed at children. Best of all, the adventure playground here is top-class, with climbing wall, water features (bring a change of clothes) and a wide range of play equipment.
SEE ALSO MUSEUMS AND GALLERIES, P.100

Salzburger Spielzeugmuseum

Bürgerspitalgasse 2; tel: 0662-62080 8300; www.salzburg museum.at; Jul–Aug, Dec: daily 9am–5pm, Sept–Nov, Jan–Jun: Tue–Sun 9am–5pm; entrance charge; map p.132 B3

The Salzburg Toy Museum exhibits a wide range of toys from ancient times to the present day, with an espe-cially notable collection of dolls, accessories and cloth-ing. There are regularly rotat-ing exhibitions which maintain variety, although the permanent collections focussing on old musical instruments, optic toys and play from the Baroque period to the 19th century are all well worth a look.

Swimming

At Bad Gastein, the Alpentherme spa complex includes a 'Family World' section, with breathtaking waterslides and the melo-dramatically named 'Black Hole Rafting' ride. Adrenalin rushes are counterpointed with the 'Lazy River', where a gentle stream leads through a

Churches

Salzburg is home to a wealth of religious architecture, whose survival is down to one man. Paris Lodron is sometimes seen as a lesser figure among the archbishops of Salzburg, calm and unassuming where others were flamboyant or, for better or worse, dramatic rulers of the prince-bishopric. However, the 'Statesman of Peace's' steady management of the province and its precarious fortunes through the Thirty Years' War is credited with the preservation of many of Salzburg's historic churches today. Elsewhere in the province are equally beautiful and historically important religious buildings.

> Note that for all churches no visits are allowed during Mass.

The Mönchsberg

The Nonnberg Convent
Nonnberggasse 2; daily
7am–dusk; map p.133 C2
The robed figures on the South Door of the church, built in 1497–9, represent Emperor Henry II (the patron of the Romanesque church), St Mary the Virgin (the church's patron saint), St Rupert and St Erentrudis. The tympanum and the lintel are relics of the Romanesque church which burned down in 1423, the ground-plan of which was maintained when rebuilding began in 1463. Some frescoes (c.1140) survived in the nuns' choir. The Chapel of St John (1448–51) has a winged altar (1498) thought to have been painted by an artist who worked with Veit Stoss.

The Altstadt

The Dom
Domplatz; Jan–Feb, Nov:
Mon–Sat 8am–5pm, Sun
1–5pm; Mar–Apr Oct, Dec:

Above: the Nonnberg Convent.

Mon–Sat 8am–6pm, Sun 1–6pm, May–Jul, Sept: Mon–Sat 8am–7pm, Sun 1–7pm, Aug: Mon–Sat 8am–8pm, Sun 1–8pm; map p.132 C2
Originally, Archbishop Wolf Dietrich also wanted to have the facade of the Cathedral realigned to give on to the Residenzplatz after the original building had burned down in a fire in 1598. However, his successor, Marcus Sitticus, cancelled this proposal when he commissioned his court architect, Santino Solari, to go ahead with the rebuilding. The alignment of the church remained as it had been when it was first built in 1181.

Solari was inspired by Italian church architecture. On the west side of the cathedral he erected the first post-medieval façade with twin towers north of the Alps; it became the model for many churches in the South German region. The porch is entered through three arched openings flanked by statues of SS Virgil and Rupert (outside) and SS Peter and Paul (inside). The broad, barrel-vaulted nave is flanked by rows of chapels and leads into the choir and transepts, which are arranged in a clover-leaf formation around the domed crossing. The ceiling paintings on the inside of the dome had to be reconstructed after World War II. The cathedral interior dates largely from the 17th century; of the old cathedral, only the font (1321) supported by four lions (12th-century) remains.

Dom Museum
Domplatz 1a; tel: 0662-8047 1860; www.kirchen.net/ dommuseum; May–Sept, Dec: Mon–Sat 10am–5pm, Sun

Right: the dome of the Dom and its doorway.

Left: the pilgrimage church of Maria Plain just outside the city of Salzburg.

cali. The church was dedicated in 1700 but the interior was not completed until after 1730. The interior achieves its characteristic effect by means of the oval plan of the dome and the main body of the church, as well as the subtle stucco decoration and colour scheme. The portrait of the Holy Family on the left side-altar is by Johann Michael Rottmayr (1708); all other altar paintings and the ceiling fresco (1728) were the work of Paul Troger. To the left of the main body of the church lies the Holy Staircase, built to a design based on the Scala Santa in Rome. It can be reached through the left-hand entrance door or, from the inside, via two chapels to the left of the main entrance.

Kollegienkirche
Universitätsplatz; daily 9am–6pm; map p.132 B3

The Collegiate Church is one of Johann Bernhard Fischer von Erlach's greatest masterpieces. The façade, with its protruding arched central section and flanking towers, became the model for many Baroque buildings in the South German area. The interior is surprisingly high and has an unusually rigid structural form. The far side of the

11am–6pm; entrance charge; map p.132 C2

In the Baroque oratories the Cathedral Museum displays artefacts including medieval sculptures, Baroque paintings and gold articles from the cathedral treasury. The oldest exhibit is St Rupert's 8th-century crozier.

Franziskanerkirche
Franziskanergasse/Siegmund-Haffner-Gasse; daily 6.30am–7.30pm; map p.132 C2

The city's Franciscan Church should be entered via the West Door in Sigmund-Haffner-Gasse. Walk through the dark nave of the earlier Romanesque building, dedicated in 1223, up to the Late

Gothic hall choir, which is flooded with light. The latter was begun in 1422 by the famous architect Hans von Burghausen and completed in 1460 by Stephan Krumenauer. In the middle is the high altar designed by Johann Bernhard Fischer von Erlach in 1709, which provides a worthy setting for a Late Gothic statue of the Virgin Mary (1485–98) by Michael Pacher. Above the nave is the oratory, commissioned by Wolf Dietrich von Raitenau in 1606 to link the church and the Residenz.

Kajetanerkirche
Kajetanerplatz; map p.133 C2

The Church of St Cajetan was built by Johann Caspar Zuc-

choir is in stark contrast: angels on stucco clouds hover around a Madonna wreathed in rays of light.

Müllnerkirche
Augustinergasse; daily, winter 8am–6pm, summer 8am–7pm; map p.132 B4

The Parish Church of Mülln is a Late Gothic church built in 1439–53 with an interior dating from 1738. The stucco work is characterised by delicate Baroque foliage and ribbons.

St Blasius
Getreidegasse; daily 7.30am–7.30pm; map p.132 B3

The Church of St Blasius (the Hospital Church), one of the oldest Gothic hall churches still standing (1330–50), has a gallery extending past the middle of the church, on which the patients were once able to take part in the service. One of the church's most remarkable treasures is the tabernacle containing the Sacrament, dating from 1480. Designed in the form of a church, it can be seen to the left of the high altar. Directly adjacent is the former Civic Hospital, which was founded in 1327. The lovely three-storey arcaded courtyard was built during the Renaissance. Today the hospital building houses the

Salzburger Spielzugmuseum (toy museum).
SEE ALSO CHILDREN, P.55

St Markuskirche
Franz-Josef-Kai 21; daily 9am–6pm; map p.132 B3

The former Ursuline Chapel is now known as St Mark's Church and was handed over to the Ukrainian Catholic Church in 1999. Its wedge-shaped ground-plan was a challenge for the architect, Johann Bernhard Fischer von Erlach. It was built between 1699 and 1705 after a massive landslide on 16 July 1669 had destroyed the previous building and killed 220 people. Since that date, 'mountain cleaners' tap the city's mountains every year to check for loose stones.

Michaelskirche
Residenzplatz; daily 8–11.45am, 1–6pm; map p.132 C3

This church was mentioned for the first time in 800 as the Palatinate Chapel, making it possibly the oldest church in Salzburg. Its present form developed between 1767–76.

Monastery of St Peter
Erzabtei St. Peter; daily 8am–noon, 2.30–6.30pm; map p.132 C2

The monastery was reorganised by St Rupert in about 696 and experienced its first

Right: in the Müllnerkirche.

Golden Age under St Virgil. The buildings reveal traces of every architectural epoch since then. A remarkable example of this mixture of styles can be seen in the Romanesque tower of the Monastery Church, which is surmounted by a Baroque cupola. Even the porch demonstrates that the church is basically High Romanesque. The late-Baroque transformation was carried out under Abbot Beda Seeauer (1753–86). Almost all the altar paintings are by Martin Johann Schmidt, and exhibit his characteristic style with its contrasts of light and dark. The cloisters to the north of the church are a mixture of Romanesque and Gothic styles and form part of the monastery; unfortunately they are closed to the public.

St Peter Katakomben
St-Peter-Bezirk; May–Sept: Tue–Sun 10.30am–5pm, Oct, Dec–Apr: Wed–Thur 10.30am–3.30pm, Fri–Sun 10.30am–4pm; entrance charge; 132 C2

Although there is not much inside the catacombs, they are still well worth a look for the atmosphere (see box, p.9).

Below: the catacombes at St Peter's.

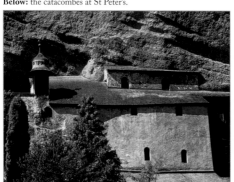

Below: the Franziskanerkirche.

The New Town

Dreifaltigkeitskirche
Makartplatz; daily 9am–5pm;
map p.132 C3

Holy Trinity Church, or, the Dreifaltigkeitskirche, enriches the Makartplatz over which its distinctive dome looms, designed by the favoured architect of the Central European Baroque, Johann Fischer von Erlach.

Kapuzinerberg Monastery
Kapuzinerberg 6; map p.132 C3

Formerly a strategically important element in the city's fortifications, this church was created to house a group of monks summoned to the city by Archbishop Wolf Dietrich in 1594. Bare and spartan, its interior reflects a sense of dedication to monastic life rather than the splendour characteristic of the city's Baroque churches.

Sebastianskirche
Linzergasse 41; daily summer: 9am–7pm, winter: 9am–4pm; map p.133 C4

The current church in this part of the New Town dates from 1820, having been previously renovated from an 1818 town fire and entirely replaced from a Gothic construction commissioned by an Archbishop in the 16th century, but torn down in 1750. Its Chapel of St Gabriel is decorated in a striking mosaic of bright, miniscule ceramic tiles. The chapel occupies part of the

adjoining cemetery, which houses the tombs of Wolf Dietrich, alchemist Paracelsus and members of the Mozart family among other famous historical figures.

Around Salzburg

Maria Plain
Plainbergweg 38, Bergheim bei Salzburg; daily, winter: 7am–5pm, summer: 7am–7pm; map p.134 C3

This famous pilgrimage church was built between 1671–4 to house a 'miraculous' portrait of the Virgin and Child. The highly decorated Baroque interior contains an altar painting by Francesco de Neve, but perhaps even more appealing are the splendid views the church's location gives over the city.

Mattsee Monastery
June–Aug: Thur–Sat 5–7pm; map p.136 C3

It is thought the monastery here was founded by Duke Tassilo of Bavaria some time after 777. Until the mid-11th century it was a Benedictine monastery; it then became a collegiate abbey. The

> The Church of Our Lady of Loreto (daily 6am–7.30pm) in Salzburg city centre was founded, along with a convent, as a home for refugee nuns fleeing Bavaria during the Thirty Years' War.

Romanesque-Gothic collegiate church acquired its present form when it was rebuilt in the Baroque style around 1700. The monastery museum contains a number of exhibits from its golden age.

Michaelbeuern Abbey
Guided tour Apr–Sept, Sun 2pm; map p.134 C4

The Benedictine abbey here is thought to have been founded in the 8th century. The Chapter Room and lower storey of the refectory date from Romanesque times. The abbey room received its stucco decorations around 1720 and is adorned with ceiling and wall paintings (c.1771). The beautiful two-storey library (1769–79) is relatively unadorned and contains 40,000 volumes. Outstanding among the 300 manuscripts is the famous Walther Bible (mid-12th century), an important example of the Salzburg book illuminator's art.

The Gothic and Baroque transformations of the abbey church were largely removed during restoration (1938–50). Some sections, including the wooden ceiling, were reconstructed in Romanesque style. The most famous item in the abbey is the high altar (1691–2), with statues by Meinrad Guggenbichler and pictures by Johann Michael Rottmayr.

Salzkammergut

St Michael's

Mondsee; daily; map p.137 C3

Most famous for its marble steps playing host to the wedding in the *The Sound of Music*, St Michael's parish church was originally part of a Benedictine monastery. Its yellow exterior and black and gold interiors recall the Habsburg era. More than half of the side altars within the church are the work of one artist, the Baroque sculptor Johannes Meinrad Guggenbichler (1649–1723). Although the church's interiors date from the 18th century, the larger institution was founded in the middle of the 8th century.

St Wolfgang
Pilgrimage Church

St Wolfgang; visits by appointment only, tel: 06138-2321; map p.135 E3

This church allegedly marks the spot where St Wolfgang's axe landed when he flung it from the overlooking mountains to determine the site of the future parish. Two very different altars by Gothic sculptor Michael Pacher (1481) and the Baroque master Guggenbichler (1706) form the key attractions of this particularly beautiful Salzkammergut

A short train ride from Gmunden lies **Traunkirchen Ort**, whose parish church (Traunkirchen Pfarrkirche; Klosterplatz 1; daily 8am–5pm) merits a brief stopover for its Fischerkanzel or Fishermen's Pulpit. Doubtless inspired by the nearby lake, the 18th-century carved wooden pulpit shows the apostles wrestling a vast catch of fish into their boat, all depicted in dramatic relief and striking colours.

church. Pacher's vast winged construction presents an interesting Gothic contrast to the Baroque work which largely replaced the medieval ornament of Austrian churches in the 18th century.

Hallstatt and Dachstein

Hallstätter Pfarrkirche und Beinhaus

Daily; entrance charge; map p.137 D1

This church on the slopes overlooking the town of Hallstatt is notable not only for its excellent views and its 1510 Gothic altar of Mary, St Catherine and St Barbara, but also for a small hut-like construction in the quiet churchyard outside. Within, are neatly arranged rows of

human remains: bones stacked in careful alignment and skulls delicately painted with ornate motifs, mottos and decoration. The effect is somewhere between sinister and kitsch yet strangely moving. This burial practice, involving the exhumation of totally decomposed bodies for transfer to the charnel house, has associations with Celtic rituals of death but in fact arose at the end of the 16th century for an entirely practical purpose: the saving of space within the limits of the tiny churchyard.

The Lammertal and Lungau

Mariapfarr Church

Mon–Fri 8am–noon; map p.139 D3

This can also lay claim to the oldest church in the Lungau to be listed in historical records (923). There is some doubt as to whether the church in question really is the parish church of Our Lady of the Assumption, but there is nonetheless no question of its great age and artistic merit. The original choir has a tower (1220) and a cycle of frescoes portraying the Life of Christ. The present altar area was added towards the end of the 14th century.

Below: the Kapuzinerberg Monastery *(see p.59).*

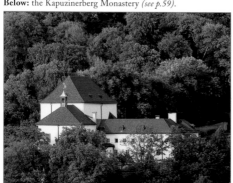

Below: St Michael's, Mondsee.

Above: the Pacher altar at St Wolfgang.

Above: St Leonhard Tamsweg.

St Leonhard

Tamsweg; daily; map p.139 E2

Allegedly the statue of St Leonhard absconded from an earlier church three times in 1421, and was found on each occasion under a juniper bush on the outskirts of the village. This was interpreted as a sign that St Leonhard wished the villagers to build a new church there; between 1424 and 1433, construction went ahead on a Late Gothic masterpiece which was surrounded by a fortifying wall in 1480. The site of St Leonhard's is, indeed, superb. It became one of the most important pilgrimage churches in Austria and is famous for its valuable interior, especially the stained-glass windows, the colours of which are particularly vivid.

St Michael im Lungau Churches

Daily; map p.139 D2

St Michael im Lungau has a remarkable concentration of churches with interesting wall paintings: the parish church of St Michael possesses the remains of frescoes dating from dating from the early 13th century to the 17th century; there is also a Roman gravestone in the North Porch. The neighbouring Chapel of St Wolfgang, in the former charnel house, has Gothic frescoes. The sister

church of St Martin in the suburb of the same name boasts a cycle of frescoes on the north outside wall dating from the first half of the 15th century; St Anne's Chapel, in the former charnel house, is adorned with late-Gothic wall paintings. The Gothic church of St Giles has a portrait of St Christopher dating from about 1400.

The Salzach and High Tauern

St Hippolytus

Zell am See; daily; map p.138 B3

St Hippolytus was originally a Romanesque-Gothic basilica which was later rebuilt. Of particular charm is the organ loft (1514–5), with elegant net vaulting and fine tracery and supported by pillars of Adnet marble.

St Maximilian

Bischofshofen; daily; map p.138 C4

The Gothic parish church of St Maximilian was built around a Romanesque core; the marble tomb of Bishop Sylvester of Chiemsee is ascribed to Hans Baldauf (1453), and is the only extant Gothic raised tomb in the Salzburg region. The Cross of St Rupert (the original of which is preserved in the priest house) was made in Ireland in about 700 and was probably brought to Salzburg during the time of St Virgil.

Mühlbach Valley

Maria Alm am Steinernen Meer

Daily; map p.138 B4

The parish and pilgrimage church here (1500–8) has the highest spire in Salzburg province; at 85m (279ft) it is taller than that of Salzburg Cathedral. The elaborate Baroque details were added during the 18th century. The portrait of the Virgin, to which are ascribed miraculous properties, is Late Gothic (1480).

The Grossglockner Hochalpenstrasse

St Vincent

Heiligenblut; daily 9am–sunset; map p.138 B2

The church here was dedicated in 1491 and the magnificent high altar was completed in 1520. It was the work of pupils of Michael Pacher (it is similar to the one in St Wolfgang). The tabernacle rises up into the roof and contains the relic of the Holy Blood of Christ, which gave the village its name, and was the reason for the church being built. Apparently, in about 900 a Danish prince received some drops of the Holy Blood as a gift from the Byzantine emperor, but died on his way back home. Three ears of corn growing out of the snow drew the locals' attention to the body, and the relic, and they built a chapel to house it.

Environment

For a country like Austria, dependent as it is on a tourism centred on the startling beauty of its natural landscapes, environmental protection is an issue of pressing self-interest. The country's many ski slopes at lower altitude, for example, are particularly threatened by global warming. Special measures have also been directed towards the preservation of water purity in Austria's lakes and the protection of the forests. These latter measures have a pragmatic function as well as supporting the tourist industry: forested slopes offer some protection against dangerous avalanches and rockfalls.

Geology

Salzburg's breathtaking landscapes are formed by its underlying geology. The city lies in part of the Alpine foothills; the region is characterised by gently rounded hills which generally reach altitudes of no more than 1,000m (3,281ft). During the Quaternary era the Salzach glacier scoured out a number of basins, some of which later became filled with water to form lakes.

The city's surrounding mountains (the Kapuzinerberg, Festungsberg, Mönchsberg, Rainberg and Hellbrunnerberg) rise from the floor of the Salzburg Basin, which gives way in the south to the limestone Alpine foothills.

The limestone High Alps, honeycombed by impressive cave systems, rise vertically from the valleys and often possess broad, undulating upland areas, as on the Untersberg, Steinernes Meer, Hochkönig, Tennengebirge and Dachstein ranges.

There are countless lakes not only in the Alpine

Above: a boundary marker to the national park.

foothills, but also in the valleys and at the foot of the high mountain ranges, but are especially prominent in the Salzkammergut.

The main valley of the Salzach divides the schistose region from the Central Alps. The water from the streams of the Tauern plunge down from the side valleys over high sills, the most dramatic of which form the Krimml Waterfalls. Over time they have eroded impressive gorges, such as the Gastein Gorge, the Kitzloch Gorge and the Liechtenstein Gorge.

The Central Alps are made up of gneiss and slate. The High Tauern consists of a series of ranges including a number of peaks of more than 3,000m (9,842ft) high. The Venediger group has the largest number of glaciers. Under the slopes of the Grossglockner (3,797m/ 12,457ft), just outside the boundaries of Salzburg province, lies the Pasterze, the longest valley glacier in Austria. Gold was once mined here in the lower Sonnblick and Goldberg mountains.

Directly to the east, framed by the Enns and Mur valleys, lie the Low Tauern. The first ranges are the Radstädter and Schladminger Tauern, which form the northern boundary of the Lungau Basin. Glaciers have left behind numerous kettle holes, in which water then collected to form little lakes.

The southern boundary of the Lungau Basin is formed by the Gurktaler Alps, whose contours are gently rounded despite their height.

Between the limestone High Alps and the Central

Left: wild flowers bloom in one of the verdant meadows that cover Salzburg Province's lowland.

replaced by those of Hitler's 'Greater Germany', but after World War II the nation returned to its typically regional approach to nature conservation. Gradually, over the latter part of the 20th century, the orientation of this approach changed from species-specific protection to a consideration of the wider habitat and local biodiversity.

In recent decades, environmental issues have responded well to the contemporary Austrian values of consensus politics and committed social policy, bringing together the public, the state and industry. Regulations regarding disposal of industrial waste and control of pollutants are stringent, and investment in the field of environmental protection is high, often between two and three per cent of GDP. Contemporary conservation laws protect specific ecosystems including wetlands, meadows and glaciers as well as the more nebulous and aesthetically defined 'character of a landscape'.

In addition to these laws, which protect over 1,000

Edelweiss, this most famous of mountain flowers, is a member of the sunflower family and a popular folk remedy across Central Europe. It is associated with Alpinism in a number of European countries including Slovenia and Switzerland; however, it holds a particularly strong connection to Salzburg, which has appropriated it as a local symbol on a number of occasions, most recently an unsuccessful bid for the 2014 Winter Olympics.

tions of conservation and sustainability is a long one, dating back to a 1524 edict by which forestry was controlled to ensure a lasting supply of timber for the local mining industry. While this was an economic, rather than ecological or aesthetic consideration, the year 1886 would see the increasingly tourism-dependent province introduce Austria's first law for the protection of a specific plant, the famous Edelweiss, symbolic of the region.

In the years 1939–45, Austria's provincially-based environmental laws were

Alps lies a zone of schistose rock, also known as the Grauwackenzone. The gently rounded peaks are covered with soil which is ideal for pastures and grazing lands. These hills are sometimes referred to as the 'Grass Mountains', while the limestone Alps are known as 'Stone Mountains'.

Environmental Protection

In many regards, Austrian environmental policy is well-developed and strictly enforced. Salzburg's historical association with ques-

Below: cranesbill geranium.

Below: Bavarian gentian.

63

specified sites including nature reserves and 'protected landscapes of recreational value', it is increasingly popular in Austria to sign contracts with landowners which restrict the use of countryside in private hands. An organisation known as BIOSA (Biosphere Austria), financed by a combination of private and state sponsors, consists of forest- and land-owners who voluntarily cede a proportion of their holdings for research purposes, to establish a scientific basis for future ecological intervention.

If there is a challenge remaining to Austria in the field of environmental protection, it is probably the development of a coherent network of nature reserves with adequate protection and management of the wildlife within. Emphasis on the quality of air and water, and concern for the interests of the tourist industry, have to some extent marginalised wildlife protection.

These issues, and lingering questions over industrial pollution, are unlikely to play a part in any tourist visit to Salzburg, however. As the region already counts on a highly developed network of local and international public transport and strongly supports both low-polluting motor vehicles and alternative means of getting about such as bicycles, most tourists will already find their environmental impact on their destination minimised by virtue of pre-existing

> At the national level of government, an Environmental Information Act prevents cover-ups and statistical manipulation of figures by ensuring that ordinary Austrians have open access to official data on the environment.

Austrian policies. Practitioners of outdoor sports, such as skiing, mountain biking and hiking, should always follow marked trails and obey all rules, which the provincial government has designed to accommodate environmental concerns.

Among the communities of Austria, contemporary Salzburg faces special challenges in caring for the environment, and it cannot be denied that the existence of a tourist industry with a local importance beyond even the already substantial Austrian norm creates additional pressures.

Urban Problems

Within the city itself, traffic is a particular problem. While the province's proportion of low-polluting motor vehicles is significantly above the Austrian national average, traffic volumes remain high, with consequent issues of noise and nitrogen pollution around the city and on provincial motorways. To the north of the province, away from tourist eyes, industrial areas continue to cause considerable if localised pollution, with nickel and lead soil deposits both being noted as of cause for concern. Forests are also threatened by this industrial pollution, with an above average number of trees dying from the top down, coniferous trees showing significant levels of sulphur in their needles, and

Below: lake, forest and mountains form a quintessentially Austrian landscape.

cadmium, arsenic and vanadium found to have been deposited in the soil across great distances. This said, Salzburg's groundwater is considered to be of notably good quality even within a country of which the Organisation for Economic Development has said, 'The quality of groundwater can rightly be a matter of national pride.'

Above: the Hochalpenstrasse is a good place to see marmots.

International Concerns

Given Austria's common borders – with no less than eight countries – rendering it susceptible to contamination from abroad, internationalism is an important element of this land-locked Central European nation's approach to environmental protection. Here, too, Salzburg is making its contribution: a research project, 'Landscape Monitoring and Nature Conservation', run from the city's university, is currently investigating the best monitoring and control techniques to protect declining biodiversity across Europe by implementing EU-wide directives.

Hydro-Electric Power

Electricity from hydro-electric projects can be controversial given the massive remodelling of the landscape it usu-

Information and maps for the the Hohetauern National Park are available from the tourist information offices of the communities within the park boundaries (Bad Gastein, Bramberg, Fusch, Hollersbach, Hüttschlag, Kaprun, Krimml, Mittersill, Mühr, Neukirchen, Rauris, Uttendorf and Wald). You can also contact the National Park Administration: Gerlos Strasse 18, 5730 Mittersill; tel: 06562 408 490; www.hohetauern.at.

ally entails; a serious bone of contention ever since economic necessity and increasing concern about the conservation of nature began to clash with each other. However, the two Tauern power-station reservoirs at Uttendorf do at least provide an enchanting view. The first discussions concerning this project, which was to become a watchword for Austrian development after the two world wars, were actually held in 1929. In 1944 the main power station in Kaprun with the auxiliary Wasserfallboden reservoir was commissioned. Eight years later, the power station linked to the Mooserboden and Margaritze were added. In 1955 the upper section with the Wasserfallboden reservoir was completed.

Hohetauern National Park

Amongst Austria's federal Bundesländer, Salzburg has the greatest proportion of national parkland, the Höhe Tauern alone forms more than a 10th of the province's area, and includes within its more than 800 sq km vast areas left entirely untouched by humankind.

The Stubach Valley was the starting-point for the idea of a High Tauern National

Park, first proposed at the beginning of this century. During the 1970s, however, it was already too late to integrate the valley into the protected area, since the energy industry had radically changed the landscape. What remained, however, was the Wiegenwald, a forest of stone pines dotted with moorland lakes. Untouched for centuries, this unspoilt biotope may be entered only in the company of a guide.

The major tourist development of the Hohetauern National Park is the Hochaplenstrasse. To the west and east of the road, the natural surroundings are strictly protected. Each year, over 1 million visitors come to gaze down on to the Pasterze Glacier. This has lead to the calls for quotas to be set to on the number of visitors in order to keep the environmental damage to a minimum. A public bus runs several times a day runs from Zell am See via Bruck up to the Franz-Josephs-Höhe and (by changing) on to Heiligenblut (and back).

Apart from the magnificent views, a notable attraction of the road is the fact that, in traversing it, one passes through a number of climatic zones, each with their corresponding types of vegetation.

65

Essentials

Salzburg is a very safe and easy city to negotiate, with all the facilities you would expect of a rich European nation. You should encounter very few problems during your stay – particularly as so much of the local economy is depedent on and geared towards keeping tourists happy – and many local people speak English and are generally willing to help if you need advice or directions. The English-language website of the city tourism authority (www.salzburg.info) is an excellent source of information and the two information offices are helpful and friendly.

Climate

Salzburg has a well-deserved reputation for being a rainy city and the watery weather even has a nickname: *Schnürlregen* (string-rain). It can rain for three seasons of the year, and in winter it snows instead. Salzburg can be exceedingly cold in winter and stiflingly hot in summer. The best times of year for visiting the city in pleasant temperatures are spring and autumn, and at these times the streets are not filled to bursting point with tourists. December, when the Christmas Market is in full swing, is also a good time, but it is much busier.

Whatever the time of year, it is always best to bring layers and something water-proof. It may be freezing cold outside in winter, but the buildings are all very well heated and insulated inside. There can be cold snaps in summer, so light jumpers or jackets can be useful.

Austrians dress casually for most occasions, although they do like to be smart when going to the theatre, opera or ballet or a ball. Evening dress is often worn to festival performances so come prepared.

Emergency Numbers

Police: tel: 133
Fire: tel: 122
Ambulance (rescue vehicle): tel: 144
Emergency medical service (Sat, Sun and public holidays only): tel: 141

Health

The health service in Salzburg is excellent. There are numerous medical facilities, including the **Unfahlkrankenhaus** on Dr-Franz-Rehrl-Platz 5 (tel: 0662-65 800; www.ukh-salzburg.at) and the **Krankenhaus der Barmherzige Brüder** (Kajetanerplatz 1; tel: 0662-80 880; www.barmherzige-brueder.at).

The *Föhn* is an atmospheric condition created by dry, warm winds which blow in to Salzburg from the base of the Alps. Residents blame everything from headaches and general ill temper to an elevated crime rate on the aggravating effects of the *Föhn*.

The Unfallkrankenhaus is renowned for treating injured Austrian skiers.

Austria and the UK have a reciprocal agreement for hospital treatment. EU citizens should arrive armed with a European Health Insurance Card (EHIC), available from post offices and online, which entitles them to reduced-cost, sometimes free, medical care.

Information

City of Salzburg Tourist Board
Auerspergstrasse 6, 5020 Salzburg; tel: 0662-889 870; www.salzburg.info; map p.132 B4

Salzburg Regional Tourist Board
Wiener Bundesstrasse 23, 5300 Hallwang bei Salzburg;

Metric to Imperial Conversions
Metres–Feet 1=3.28
Kilometres–Miles 1=0.62
Hectares–Acres 1=2.47
Kilogrammes–Pounds 1=2.2
°C–°F 0°=32° (double the figure and add 30)

Left: come prepared for *Schnürlregen*.

Salzburg Card

If you are planning in cramming in a lot in a short space of time then the Salzburg Card might be useful, available online (www.salzburginfo.at), at information offices, from hotels and at the airport. Available for 24, 48 or 72 hours, it costs between €22 and €35 and is half price for children (up to 15 years). As well as gaining you free access to nearly all the sights in the city it also allows free travel on the city's public transport.

Telephones

Telephone calls may be made from post offices and from public call-boxes. Most public telephones require telephone cards (sold in various denominations at post offices).

The international dialling code for Austria is 43, and the area code for Salzburg is 0662. To make an international call from Austria, dial 00 + the international code.

Below: post boxes are yellow.

tel: 0662-66880; www.salzburgerland.com
Salzkammergut Tourism
Salinenplatz 1, 4820 Bad Ischl; tel: 06132-26909; www.salzkammergut.at; map p.137 D2
Tourist information offices in Salzburg are at Mozartplatz 5 and the railway station.

Media

Apropos and Kultplan

Apropos (www.apropos.or.at) is a punchy alternative newspaper sold on the streets, with news, comment, a critical insight into social issues and good listings too, if you can read German. Half of the cover price goes to the vendor. To find out what bands are playing or which club nights are going on every month, pick up the local free listings sheet *Kultplan* (www.kultplan.at), widely available from cafés and bars.

Money

The currency in Austria is the euro (€). 1 euro equals 100 cents. Banknotes are available in denominations of 500, 200, 100, 50, 20, 10 and 5 euros. There are coins for 2

and 1 euro, and for 50, 20, 10, 5, 2 and 1 cent.

The most favourable exchange rate is at banks (avoid the *bureaux de change*), and ATMs can be found at many banks all over the city. Most international credit cards are accepted in banks, major hotels and restaurants, and in the majority of shops in the city centre.

Post

Salzburg's main post office is at Residenzplatz 9. Post offices are generally open Mon–Fri 8am–noon, 2–6pm, some are also open Sat 8–10am (see www.post.at). Stamps can also be bought at tobacconists.

Public Holidays

1 January; 6 January (Epiphany); Easter Monday; 1 May; Ascension Day; Whit Monday; Corpus Christi; 15 August (Assumption of the Virgin Mary); 26 October (National Holiday); 1 November (All Saints); 8 December (Annunciation); 25–26 December (Christmas).

Festivals

That Salzburg is a city of the arts is beyond doubt. As well as being the birthplace of one of the greatest of all European composers, it is also the location of the world's most famous festival of music and drama; the Salzburger Festspiele. Founded by Max Reinhardt and Hugo von Hofmannsthal in 1920, it has attracted some of the greatest names in 20th century music, including Richard Strauss, Arturo Toscanini, Herbert von Karajan and Claudio Abbado. However, the music continues all year, with other festivals dedicated to works of Mozart, jazz and contemporary avant garde music and dance.

History

The centenary celebrations of Mozart's birth in 1856 were held in honour of a composer who had once been literally kicked out of the service of Prince-Bishop Hieronymus Colloredo, and who 'cared very little for Salzburg' (to use one of his less colourful expressions). The Cathedral Music Association and Mozarteum had been founded as early as 1841.

This body was later to evolve into the International Mozarteum Foundation, devoted to the furthering of and research into Mozart's music, along with the Mozarteum Academy of Music and Dramatic Art. During the following decades, a succession of large-scale musical celebrations was held in Salzburg.

Like all parts of the Austro-Hungarian Empire, Salzburg was drawn into the 1914–18 war which erupted in the wake of the assassination of the Habsburg heir Franz Ferdinand in Sarajevo. In the wake of the Habsburg defeat, Salzburg was

Above: a poster for the annual festival of Mozart's music.

assigned to the Democratic Republic of Austria by yet another international map-drawing exercises at Versailles. The new republic experienced two decades of turmoil as the Red and Black of left and right wing forces struggled to assert themselves in the insecure new polity. The Salzburg Festival, created by Hugo von Hofmannsthal and others in the immediate wake of imperial defeat represented a major creative effort to

bolster the identity of the shattered Austrian rump state in the wake of the Versailles dissection through conservative 'high culture'.

The First Festival

The spark of genius needed to get this moving was supplied by the theatre producer Max Reinhardt, who came up with the idea of a Salzburg Festival. 'Here, where the eye delights everywhere it looks, where every glimpse encounters exquisite harmony, where an entire city reveals beauty in its innermost being; here is the right place to celebrate a festival,' he pronounced. In 1917 he presented his plans for the organisation of a festival as well as the erection of a festival hall.

The same year saw the founding of the Salzburg Festival Community. On its artistic committee sat leading artists of the time: Max Reinhardt, the conductor Franz Schalk, the composer Richard Strauss, the poet Hugo von Hofmannsthal and the set-designer Alfred Roller. In spite of financial difficulties

Left: the first performance of *Jedermann* in 1920.

extended by the addition of new buildings and reconstruction of old ones to create today's festival complex. Closely linked with the name of the architect, Clemens Holzmeister, the Small and Large Festival Halls and the open-air stage of the Summer Riding School (built directly into the mountainside) extend behind the long façade of the former princely stables.

The festival completely transformed Salzburg during the 1920s. The little town in which Stefan Zweig had chosen to live 'above all because of its romantic remoteness' became during the course of just a few years one of the great cultural centres of Europe. 'I have many happy memories of the Salzburg of the late 1920s and early 1930s, when it was a mecca for many artists, a unique blend of the spirit of Mozart and the most modern and daring trends in music, art, theatre and stage design,' reminisced Robert Stolz. The festival's typical style of performance was determined above all by Max Reinhardt, Bruno Walter and Arturo Toscanini.

The resident orchestra of the Salzburger Festspeile is the renowned Wiener Philharmoniker (Vienna Philharmonic, www.wienerphilharmoniker.at). Founded in 1842, it has a pedigree unrivalled by any other orchestra. Its conductors have included Gustav Mahler, Richard Strauss, Bruno Walter and Karl Böhm.

The 1920s and 30s

In 1922, Hofmannsthal's *Great Salzburg World Theatre* received its premiere in the Collegiate Church. In addition, an opera was performed for the first time in the Regional Theatre: Mozart's *Don Giovanni*. In the same year the foundation stone was laid for the Festival Hall in Hellbrunn Park, but unfortunately there was no money to complete the project. In 1924, it was decided to use part of the princely stables for the project. Over the decades, this makeshift solution was

and planning problems, particularly after the collapse of the Danube monarchy in 1918, the festival opened in 1920 with a performance of Hofmannsthal's *Jedermann* (Everyman) under the direction of Max Reinhardt.

The actors performed without fees, with the exception of Werner Krauss, who played Death and the Devil; he insisted on payment in the form of a pair of Salzburg *Lederhosen*. The mystery play of the life and death of a rich man, performed in front of the perfect setting of the west front of the cathedral, rapidly gained in popularity and became an essential part of the festival.

Below: the façade of the Festival Halls, designed by Clemens Holzmeister.

Postwar Festivals

The Anschluss of Austria with the German Reich in 1938 put an end to the work of these and many other artists, when the Salzburg Festival was appropriated by the Nazi propaganda machine. However, during the postwar years, the names of other great artists were associated with outstanding performances.

In 1960 Herbert von Karajan opened the Large Festival Hall with a performance of the opera *Der Rosenkavalier* by Richard Strauss and Hugo von Hofmannsthal, and up until his death in 1989, Karajan's influence was to decisively shape the future of the festival. which is currently run by Jürgen Flimm.

The Mozarteum

In 1848, the International Mozarteum Foundation was formed to 'perform and propagate Mozart's music'. Today, the Foundation runs two museums in the city. Its collections include the composer's original letters and sheet music and numerous recorded performances of his work.

The Foundation is best known for its two long-running concert series. Mozart Week (Mozartwoche)

> Every year, on the first and second weekend in August, the Hellbrunn Festival is held at the *Schloss,* featuring operas, plays and concerts.

is held in late January, with a 10-day presentation of the composer's works to mark his birthday on 27 January. Performances often include concerts by the Vienna Philharmonic Orchestra and concertos by star pianists. In summer, the Foundation's concert series forms a key part of the Salzburg Festival.

The headquarters of the Mozarteum are behind the Landestheater, as are the departments of the College of Music and Dramatic Arts. During July and August conducted tours are available through the concert and college building, which were built between 1910 and 1914 in neoclassical, neo-Baroque and Secessionist style.

Also in the tour are visits to Mozart's apartment and the Magic Flute Cottage, a summer house in which Mozart is supposed to have composed his famous last opera. It originally stood in Vienna near the Theater an der Wien, but was donated to the city of Salzburg in 1873.

Festival Listings

MOZARTWOCHE

Stiftung Mozarteum, Schwarzstrasse 26, 5020 Salzburg; tel: 0662-889 400 154; www.mozarteum.at; map p.132 C3

This festival, given over in part to the works of Mozart, is run by the Mozarteum, the organisation that promotes his music, and also includes the works of contemporary composers. It takes place in late-Jan to Feb around the time of the composer's birthday.

OSTERFESTSPIELE SALZBURG

Herbert-von-Karajan-Platz 9, 5020 Salzburg; tel: 0662-8045 361; www.osterfestspiele-salzburg.at; map p.132 B3

Salzburg's Easter Festival has just finished a cycle of *Der Ring des Nibelungen* under Simon Rattle with the Berliner Philharmoniker. Future plans include a new production of Strauss's *Salome.*

Below: the composer Richard Strauss.

Below: Hugo von Hofmannsthal.

Left: a performance of *Der Rosenkavalier* at the Festival.

sheets that tell you what tickets are still available for each performance. It is possible to buy tickets in advance on-line. Once you have made your purchase you will receive a notification of this in the post and the tickets will appear a couple of weeks later.

Guided tours are available of the backstage of the Festival Halls, usually off-limits to non-performers, at 2pm daily, also 3.30pm June–Sept and 9.30am July–Aug.

SALZBURGER JAZZ HERBST
Ticket Office: Gusshausstrasse 23/18, 1040 Wien; tel: 01-504 8500; www.salzburgerjazz herbst.at; Mon–Fri 10am–4pm
This is Salzburg's annual jazz festival. It attracts big, international names and takes place for two weeks at the end of Oct/beginning Nov.

SALZBURGER PFINGST-FESTSPIELE
Herbert-von-Karajan-Platz 11, A-5020 Salzburg; tel: 0662-8045 500; www.salzburgfestival.at; map p.132 B3
This is the Whitsun festival, linked to the main summer Festspiele. Run by Riccardo Muti with his Orchestra Giovanile 'L. Cherubini', they are currently concentrating on known works by Italian composers of the 18th century, especially those from Naples.

SZENE SALZBURG
Republic, Anton-Neumayr-Platz 2, 5020 Salzburg; tel: 0662-843 448; www.szene-salzburg.net; map p.132 B3
In June and July Salzburg's annual festival of contemporary art, music and dance takes place in its own theatre, Republic.

SALZBURGER ADVENTSINGEN
Ticket Office: Residenzplatz 9, 5010 Salzburg; tel: 0662-843 182; www.salzburgeradventsin gen.at; map p.132 C3
High kitsch indeed, but one guaranteed to bring a lump into the throat of most Salzburgers. This is a special carol concert held in the Grossen Festspielhaus.

SALZBURGER FESTSPIELE
This is the city's main festival of music and theatre featuring world-famous performers such as the Wiener Philharmoniker, the resident orchestra of the festival. Under artistic director Jürgen Flimm, and starting with a performance of Hofmannsthal's *Jedermann* on the Dom steps, it takes over the city from the end of July to the end of August every year.
Kartenbüro der Salzburger Festspiele
Herbert-von-Karajan-Platz 11;

postal address: Postfach 140, 5010 Salzburg, Austria; tel: 0662-8045 500; www. salzburgfesti val.at; daily 10am–6pm during the Festival; map p.132 B3
The helpful main ticket office is just across the road from the Festival Halls, by the Siegmundstor. During the festival the organisers put out a daily free newspaper (pick it up at the Festival Halls) giving reviews and what is to happen that day. Also look out for the free

In late-2009 and early-2010 the Salzburg Easter Festival was rocked by scandal, with allegations of massive fraud (of over 2 million euros), the disappearance of the festival's executive director amid accusations of embezzlement, and the apparent attempted suicide of the festival's technical director. The Austrian police say it will take a long time to uncover the full extent of the crime.

Film

F ilm in Salzburg means, of course, one thing
above all: *The Sound of Music*. Robert Wise's
1965 film of the Rodgers and Hammerstein
musical made an unlikely international success
story. Despite a tale and setting that have come
to seem essentially Austrian, the film has been
historically ill-received in the country. Indeed,
the production's history indicates its estrangement
from Austria in many ways: this American film
was derived from a Broadway musical and
inspired by a German adaptation of Maria Von
Trapp's book. That said, it remains one of the
most popular films of all time.

The Sound of Music

The story of the novice Maria,
her appointment as nanny to
the Von Trapp family, and her
subsequent winning over of
children and father alike with
song, is a favourite across the
English-speaking world
which, for all its kitsch, has
risen to the heights of the cinematic canon. If the movie
itself is an airy confection as
light as the meringue-like
Nockerln dessert for which
the city is famous, its origins
in a true story of the early 20th
century, and its subsequent
success as a worldwide representation of the Austrian
nation, make it a highly significant cultural phenomenon.

The Sound of Music proj-
ect had its origins in two German films adapted fom the
autobiography of Maria von
Trapp. After theatre director

Apocryphally, the British
government holds audio and
video copies of *The Sound of
Music* in their archives as
morale-boosting material to be
broadcast in the wake of a
national emergency.

Above: Christopher Plummer,
like the majority of Austrians,
is said to have hated *The
Sound of Music*.

Vincent J. Donehue saw the
films, he and producers
Leland Hayward and Richard
Halliday designed a stage
production around actress
Mary Martin as Maria. Halliday, conveniently, was Martin's own husband. The star's
desire for original songs to be
written for her character led
to the initial intention, a stage
play incorporating traditional
music from the Von Trapp
repertoire, to evolve into the
ne plus ultra of Rodgers and
Hammerstein musicals we
know today. Premiering in

1959 on the Broadway stage,
the film adaptation, scripted
by old Hollywood hand and
Hitchcock collaborator
Ernest Lehman, followed in
1965 and swiftly became one
of the all-time box office hits
of North American cinema.
Robert Wise won the Oscar
for his direction in addition to
the production's four other
Academy Awards, including
Best Picture. Lead actress
Julie Andrews was unsuc-
cessful in her nomination, but
Maria remains one of her
most famous roles.

The historical and geo-
graphical inaccuracies of the
film, which blend Austrian
locations with Bavarian ones
and compress the Von Trapp
story of romance and escape
into a single year, have only
made it more powerful as a
symbol of Austria to the
wider world in the 20th century and beyond. While it
might be an innocent error for
foreigners to take Oscar
Hammerstein's 'Edelweiss'
for a traditional Austrian tune,
it is more serious to consider
how the movie served to
cement a positive image of

Left: all together now, 'Do, a deer…'

the Ebensee, among other locations, standing in for Bavaria under Nazi rule. By 1980, Salzburg was allowed to represent itself in English-speaking cinema, when Walther Matthau's whistle-blower agent fled there in the mediocre CIA comedy-drama *Hopscotch*, although some critics may wish that he had not bothered.

Das Kino

Giselakai 11; tel: 0662-873 100; www.daskino.at; map p.132 C3

Among Salzburg's film venues, one cinema deserves special mention. Das Kino, in the New Town, is an excellent arts and rep cinema, well equipped and furnished with comfortable, ergonomically designed seating. It is a member of the Network for European Film, supporting the continent's filmmakers but also holding seasons of Latin American and other world productions. There is an extensive selection of arts magazines and promotional flyers in the foyer for those seeking the latest listings.

Amongst those supposed to have been considered for various roles in the film are Yul Brynner and Richard Burton for the Captain, Doris Day and Audrey Hepburn for Maria, and the elder Osmond brothers for the Von Trapp boys.

larly good year for the city on film: in addition to *The Sound of Music*, the region also served as backdrop to Natalie Wood and Tony Curtis' adventures in *The Great Race* and was chosen to represent the Swiss Alps as the refuge of the Beatles, on the run from malevolent mystics in *Help!*. Three years later, Clint Eastwood and Richard Burton's elaborate espionage double-cross in *Where Eagles Dare* involved

Austrians as innocent victims of Nazism. This image was far from the whole story and widely obscured the histories of persecution and anti-Semitism perpetrated by Austrians, which actually characterised the period covered in the film. Discomfort with the legacy of Nazism in Germany and Austria themselves was so strong that early releases reputedly cut the final act of the film, so that the story ended with the Von Trapps' wedding.

Other Efforts

Of course Maria and company are not Salzburg's sole contribution to cinematic culture, although the province is best known as a location rather than a filmmakers' haven. 1965 was a particu-

Below: the original von Trapp family singers.

Food and Drink

Hearty, filling and delicious, Austrian food rarely strays far from a basic regional menu, at least outside the capital. This certainly holds true for Salzburg, where traditional gastronomy has a key part to play in attracting the city's many thousands of yearly visitors. From 'Salzburger Nockerl' to Stiegl beer and goulash to garlic soup, Salzburg has many local delights which stand out even among Austrian cuisine with its uniformly high standards. Not traditionally friendly for vegetarians, an influx of new dishes means that non-meat eaters can usually find something tasty to eat.

What to Eat

Austrian breakfasts *(Frühstücke)* almost always involve bread rolls being served with tea or coffee, the accompaniments varying with price of venue from jam and pâté to fresh fruit, cold meats, cheeses and hot options.

More important to the Austrian stomach is lunch, or *Mittagessen*, which often forms the main meal of the day. Many locals eat from the *Mittagsmenu* or the *Tagesmenu*. These set menus offer better value for money, although evening meals at restaurants *(Abendessen)* will offer a wider range of dishes.

International cuisine has made less impact on Salzburg than other Austrian cities, tending only to an Italian influence on mainstream restaurants and a smattering

Above: local cheese can be excellent.

of Asian cuisine. For those on the go, Austria remains the patron nation of the cake in all its forms, with Torte and Kuchen hearty enough to serve as a meal.

These are often taken with a coffee; although the *Kaffeehaus* culture cannot match that of Vienna, Salzburg nonetheless has its fair share of these venerable institutions, with their own special vocabulary:

Schwarzer or Mocca: black coffee, ask for the drink *verlängerter* if you would prefer a weaker serving.

Although the situation has improved greatly for vegetarians in recent years, vegan travellers in particular may still struggle to meet their dietary requirements in today's Salzburg. Help and advice can be obtained from the Österreichischer Vegetarier-Union (Postfach 1, 8017 Graz; tel: 0316-463 717; www.vegetarier.at), and the Vegane Gesellschaft Österreich (Waidhausenstrasse 13/1, 1140 Wien; tel: 01-9291 4988; www.vegan.at).

Brauner: ordered *Grosse* ('large') or *Kleine* ('small'), a coffee with a little milk or cream.

Melange: large cappucino-like milky coffee.

Einspänner: a *Schwarzer* served with whipped cream.

Cappucino: deceptively named, this is in fact a *Brauner* topped with whipped cream.

If a savoury snack option is preferred, sausage stalls offer the spicy Bosna and Debreziner, the cheese-speckled Käsekrainer, and

In 2005, to commemorate the 50th anniversary of the Austrian State Treaty and the end of postwar occupation, the Salzburger Kokos-Rollen, a 1950s coconut sweet, was revived for Austrian shoppers.

Left: a handsome piece of *Speck*.

gifts and seasonal baked goods. Locals will use this for staples of high quality; fresh bread, fish, poultry and meats as well as fine artisan-made cheeses and other local produce. Open from early in the morning until lunchtime.

Bäckerei Funder
Linzergasse 2, tel: 0662-874 479; Mon–Sat; map p.132 C3
Josef Funder are bakers with flair. Their loaves baked into the shape of rabbits and lambs, which are sold at Easter, are works of art.

Confiserie Josef Holzermayr
Alter Markt 7; tel: 0662-842 365; www.holzermayr.at; Mon–Sat 9am–6pm, Sun 10am–7pm; map p.132 C3
A long-standing sweet shop with better than average Mozart balls.

Flöckner
Mirabellplatz 7a; tel: 0662-871 438; www.floeckner.at; Mon–Fri 6.15am–6pm, Sat 7.30am–noon, Sun 8am–4pm; map p.132 C4

the self-explanatory Currywurst in addition to the Bratwurst and frankfurters more familiar to foreign palates. Austrian supermarkets are also excellent resources for picnic food, supplying fresh fruit, cold cuts and baked goods in abundance.

Local Dishes

Salzburg is particularly known for sweets and confectionery. The *Mozartkugel*, a ball of marzipan and chocolate, today virtually serves as a marker for Austrian identity and has even been taken as the subject of serious sociological research. In the home town of Mozartmania, of course, it is sold by the barrel-load. Equally delightful, and thankfully a good deal lighter, are the bilberry soufflés and Salzburger Nockerl – light concoctions of eggs, milk, sugar, butter and flour – which you will find on many local menus.

Among savoury dishes, garlic soups are a speciality of the province, as are beef braised in beer and veal

olives. All this can be washed down with half-litre (a *Krügerl*) or third of a litre (a *Seidl*) of Stiegl, the most popular local beer.

Food Shopping

The Mirabellplatz is not only site of the Christmas markets, but also Thursday's regular Schrannemarkt of food and crafts ranging from hand made flower arrangements to

Below: the Salzburger Nockerl, a soufflé of impressive proportions.

A usefully situated chain of bakers, this is the principal shop, excellent for picnic supplies.

Hans Erlach

Linzergasse 3; tel: 0662-874 435; Mon–Sat; map p.132 C3

This excellent New Town deli serves cold cuts and a range of Austrian specialities; plenty of pork and *Kren* (horseradish).

Magazin

Augustinergasse 13; tel: 0662-841 5840; www.magazin.co.at; Tue–Sat 10am–7.30pm; map p.132 A3

This classy, modern restaurant and wine bar has delicatessen attached that stocks an excellent selection of wines and kitchen accessories.

R.F. Azwanger

Getreidegasse 15; tel: 0662-843 3940; www.azwanger.at; Mon–Fri 10am–6pm, Sat 9.30am–5pm, Sun 10am–4pm; map p.132 B3

A traditional delicatessen with a good range of drinks.

Sporer

Getreidegasse 39; tel: 0662-845 431; www.sporer.at; Mon–Fri 9.30am–7pm, Sat 8.30am–5pm; map p.132 B3

A good place to find local schnapps and liqueurs. They open later on the Saturday before Christmas.

There are two good markets in Salzburg where you can find local produce such as cheese, hams, sausages, bread and cakes, as well as wines and schnapps. As well as the **Schrannenmarkt** (Mirabellplatz Thur 5am–1pm), the **Grünmarkt** is held in Universitätsplatz, by the Kollegienkirche, Mon–Fri 7am–7pm, Sat 6am–3pm.

Food Vocabulary

A table for one/two *Ein Tisch für eine Person/zwei Personen, bitte*
Could we order please? *Können wir bitte bestellen?*
Can we have the bill, please? *Können wir bitte bezahlen?*
Bill *Zahlen/Rechnung*
evening meal *Abendessen*
lunch *Mittagessen*
children's portion *Kinderteller*
snack *Jause, Imbiss*
menu *Speisekarte*
soup/starter *Suppe/ Vorspeise*
main course *Hauptgericht*
dessert *Nachspeise*
beer/wine *Bier/Wein*
bread *Brot*
bread roll *Brötchen, Semmel*
cake *Kuchen*
coffee *Kaffee*

---

milk *Milch*
mineral water *Mineralwasser*
mustard *Senf*
salt/pepper *Salz/Pfeffer*
sugar *Zucker*
tea *Tee*
tip *Trinkgeld*
wine list *Weinkarte*

BREAKFAST FRÜHSTÜCK
Brot bread
Semmel/Brötchen roll
Eier eggs
Fruchtsaft fruit juice
Gebäck pastries
heiss hot
kalt cold
Marmelade/Konfitüre jam
Orangensaft orange juice
Pumpernickel black rye bread
Rühreier scrambled egg
Schinken ham
Schwarzbrot brown rye bread
Speck bacon
Weissbrot white bread

SOUPS SUPPEN
Eintopf thick soup
Erbsensuppe pea soup
Fritattensuppe consommé with strips of pancake
Gemüsesuppe vegetable soup
Griessnockerlsuppe semolina dumpling soup
Gulaschsuppe goulash soup
Hühnersuppe chicken soup

Below: a famous local beer that goes down easily.

Below: …or try one of these Austrian wines…

Below: …and finish up with one of these schnapps.

Above: Austrian pastries are some of the best in the world, best washed down with a good cup of coffee..

Leberknödelsuppe consommé with liver dumplings.
Nudelsuppe noodle soup
Ochsenschwanzsuppe oxtail soup
Zwiebelsuppe onion soup

MEAT COURSES
FLEISCHGERICHTE
Backhuhn roast chicken
Beuschel a casserole of finely-chopped offal.
Blutwurst black pudding
Bockwurst large frankfurter
Bratwurst fried sausage
Currywurst pork sausage with curry powder
Stelze knuckle of pork
Ente duck
Fasan pheasant
Fleischlaibchen meatballs
Fleischpastetchen rissole
Gulasch goulash
Hähnchen/Huhn chicken
Kalbsbries veal sweetbreads
Kümmelfleisch pork stew with cumin
Lamm am Spiess lamb on the spit
Lammbraten roast lamb
Leberknödel liver dumplings
Ochsenschwanz oxtail
Räucherschinken cured ham
Rehrücken saddle of deer
Rind beef
Rinderbraten roast beef
Rinderfilet fillet of beef

Sauerbraten braised pickled beef
Schweinebauch belly of pork
Schweinebraten roast pork
Schweinefilet loin of pork
Speck bacon
Tiroler Bauernschmaus various meats with sauerkraut and dumplings
Wienerschnitzel breaded escalope of veal
Zigeunerschnitzel veal with peppers and relishes
Zunge tongue

FISH FISCH
Bismarckhering filleted pickled herring
Fischfrikadellen fishcakes
Forelle trout
Hecht pike
Heringstopf pickled herrings
Lachs salmon
Muscheln mussels

DUMPLINGS AND
NOODLES KNÖDEL
Semelknödel/Serviettenknödl bread dumplings
Leberknödel liver dumplings
Kanocken/Kässpätzle/Kasnödel dumplings with cheese
Kartoffelknödel potato dumplings
Knödel dumplings
Nockerl gnocchi
Nudeln noodles
Spätzle grated pasta

VEGETABLES GEMÜSE
Bohnen beans
Bratkartoffeln fried potatoes
Pilzen mushrooms
Erdäpfel/Kartoffel potatoes
Kartoffelsalat potato salad
Knoblauch garlic
Kohl cabbage
Kopfsalat lettuce
Linsen lentils
Pommes (frites) chips
Rohnen beetroot
Sauerkraut pickled cabbage

DESSERTS NACHSPEISEN
Apfelkuchen apple cake
Apfelstrudel apple pastry
Eis ice cream
Kaiserschmarrn sugared pancake with raisins
Käsetorte cheesecake
Linzer Torte cake spread with jam topped with cream
Marillenknödel apricot dumplings
Mandelkuchen almond cake
Mohnkuchen poppyseed cake
Obstkuchen fruit tart
Palatschinken pancakes
Pofesen stuffed fritters
Rote Grütze raspberries or redcurrants with semolina
Sacher Torte chocolate cake with jam and chocolate
Schwarzwälder Kirschtorte Black Forest gateau

77

History

4000 BC
Rainberg settlement.

800–400 BC
Arrival of the Celts. Salt mines are dug.

15 BC
Romans conquer Noricum. Foundation of Salzburg as Juvavum.

AD 45
Juvavum becomes an official town on a strategic road route.

c.500
Romans withdraw from Noricum.

696
Bishop Rupert of Worms is awarded Salzburg, founding St Peter's Abbey and the Nonnberg convent.

739
Salzburg becomes a bishopric.

774
The first cathedral is consecrated.

798
Charlemagne uses his influence to have the pope promote Salzburg to an archbishopric.

1077
Construction begins on the Hohensalzburg Fortress.

1167
The city is burned to the ground by Emperor Barbarossa, having sided with the pope against him.

1190
Salt mining revives and with it the city's economic fortunes.

1348
Plague arrives in Salzburg, with massive loss of life.

c.1400
Imperial influence increases in the city, causing the archbishops' power to wane.

1498
The city's Jewish population is expelled by Archbishop von Keutschach.

1511
Rights granted to the city government by the empire are rescinded after more than a century under pressure from the church.

1612
Archbishop Wolf Dietrich abdicates after a failed coup, leaving as his legacy a quarter of a century of investment in the city's Baroque architecture.

1623
Paris Lodron, archbishop, founds the city's university.

1756
Mozart is born in the city on 27 January.

1781

Mozart leaves under a cloud after clashing with the archbishop.

1800

Napoleon's troops briefly take Salzburg.

1803

Imperial authority brings a definitive end to the clerical state.

1816

Salzburg is incorporated into the Habsburg Empire.

1861

Salzburg receives its own regional government, with parliamentary elections.

1914–8

Salzburg, as part of the Habsburg Empire, is drawn into the conflict that will become World War I. In the subsequent negotiations at Versailles, it is decided that it will join the territory of the new Austrian nation.

1920

Salzburg formally made a province of the Austrian republic. Year of the first Salzburg festival.

1938

German troops enter Austria following the referendum over Anschluss.

1945

US troops enter Salzburg after a year of heavy bombing.

1955

The Austrian State Treaty marks the end of occupation and the re-emergence of independent Austrian government on the principle of strict neutrality.

1962

Paris Lodron University reopens.

1997

The Old Town is recognised as a World Heritage Site by Unesco.

2006

The 250th anniversary of Mozart's birth is celebrated in Salzburg and Vienna.

2010

The Salzburg Easter Festival is rocked by scandal as evidence of massive fraud is uncovered.

Hotels

Salzburg offers a wide selection of accommodation for all tastes and budgets. There are some wonderful luxury hotels in historic buildings, but there is also a wealth of smaller, more individual places, especially outside of the centre. Outside of the city centre prices can be very reasonable for what is offered and there are some fabulous spa hotels where you can be pampered to within an inch of your life. Prices vary depending on the season. If you are visiting Salzburg either during the Salzburg Festival or during Christmas and New Year, it is highly recommended you book well in advance.

Mönchsberg

Schloss Mönchstein
Mönchsberg Park 26; tel: 0662-8485 550; www.monchstein.com; €€€; bus 7, 20, 21, 24, 27, 28; map p.132 B3
Situated on top of the Mönchsberg and surrounded by a park, this is one of the finest and most exclusive hotels in the city. The individually decorated bedrooms and bathrooms are out of this world. Needless to say, the location offers some of the best views of the city. Early booking is essential.

Altstadt

Altstadthotel Kasererbräu
Kaigasse 33; tel: 0662-842 4450; www.kasererbraeu.at; €; map p.133 C2
A charming, central hotel on Kaigasse. The rooms have a medieval feel about them and feature antique furniture,

including solid wooden beds. Surprisingly, for a small central hotel, it features a luxurious wellness facility that includes a sauna and a Turkish bath.

Altstadthotel Weisse Taube
Kaigasse 9; tel: 0662-842 404; www.weissetaube.at; €; map p.133 C2
Managed by the Wollner family, this traditional hotel is in the pedestrianised part of the Old Town, right next to Mozartplatz. It was built in 1365, on land belonging to St Peter's Abbey. Although the rooms are not particularly of any era or theme, they are basic and comfortable. Breakfast room and bar, but no restaurant.

Ambiente Hotel Struber
Nonntaler Hauptstrasse 35; tel: 0662-843 728; www.struber.at; €; bus: 5, 25; map p.133 C1
Located in the Nonntal district, behind the Old Town. Just 14 rooms, some with wooden beams, all with a rustic charm. Some have balconies with views of the fortress. Delicious home cooking.

Arthotel Blaue Gans
Getreidegasse 41–3; tel: 0662-

8424 9150; www.blauegans.at; €€€; map p.132 B3
The 'Blue Goose Art Hotel' calls itself a 'habitable work of art', and successfully fuses traditional and modern styles. The 38 rooms feature interesting works of art, crisp fabrics and warm lighting, all in a building that's nearly 700 years old.

Hotel Elefant
Sigmund-Haffner-Gasse 4; tel: 0662-843 397; www.elefant.at; €–€€; map p.132 C3
Over 700 years old, and located very centrally in the Old Town, in an alleyway off the shopping street Getreidegasse. There is a curious story that King Max of Bavaria had an elephant which stopped to look in the window of the building, since when it has been known as Elefant. The rooms are quite simple, though they are comfortable with subtle styling. There are two restaurants and the 17th-century Ratsherrnkeller. Parents may find the child care facilities, permitting an hour or two for themselves, particularly appealing.

Left: reception at the Goldener Hirsch.

fast is laid on downstairs and the staff are friendly and helpful. A bargain so close to the main sights.

New Town

Adlerhof

Elisabethstrasse 25; tel: 0662-875 236; www.gosalzburg.com; €; bus: 1, 2, 3, 4, 5, 25, 840
Shared or private bathrooms are on offer at this budget pension, which is located a little too far north of town for easy exploring but useful for those making a quick stopover or departing at an awkward hour, as the train station is right alongside.

Austrotel

Paris-Lodron-Strasse 1; tel: 0662-881 688; www.austrotel. at; €€; bus: 1, 2, 3, 5, 6, 25, 840; map p.132 C4
Major-league four star hotel in North American style. Although the building was once home to Archbishop Paris Lodron, the interior has been thoroughly modernised. Amongst the staff, Austrian good manners are leavened with a refreshingly

Hotel Goldene Ente

Goldgasse 10; tel: 0662-845 622; www.ente.at; €; map p.132 C3
A very central location in the Old Town, based on one of Salzburg's oldest (14th-century) inns. Rooms are decorated in the style of traditional country homes, with antiques and art on the walls. The restaurant is a favourite haunt of the locals, which means it has good traditional cooking.

Hotel Goldener Hirsch

Getreidegasse 37; tel: 0662-80 840; www.starwoodhotels.com; €€€; map p.132 B3
Set in a building dating back to 1407, this is the finest hotel in the Altstadt, much beloved of stars visiting the Festival who appreciate its discrete luxury. All the rooms are unique, with their own colour schemes and themes reminiscent of a 15th-century inn, combining antique furniture and modern amenities. The service, as you would expect, is excellent and there is a very fine restaurant attached to the hotel serving traditional Austrian food.

Star Inn Hotel

Hildmannplatz 5; tel: 0662-846 846; www.starinn.at; €; bus: 1, 4; map p.132 B3
Set just the other side of the Sigmundstor, less than 5 min walk from the Altstadt, this great value hotel opened Only a few years ago. The large, airy rooms are spotlessly clean and refeshingly free of clutter. A bonus is the large windows that let in lots of natural light. A good break-

Below: the rather kitsch pile of Schloss Mönchstein.

Below: designer comfort at the Blaue Gans.

Above: the bar of the Goldener Hirsch, *see p.81.*

cheery sense of humour. The rooms are spacious and exquisitely, if conservatively, furnished. There is a ground floor lounge in which guests are provided with free soft drinks.

Crowne Plaza Pitter
Rainerstrasse 6; tel: 0662-889 780; www.crowneplaza.com; €€€; bus: 1, 2, 3, 4, 5, 6, 25, 840; map p.132 B4

An excellent hotel whose elegant interior décor pays tribute to the late-19th century origins of the building, with a particularly eye-catching wood-panelled dining room. Traditional, but with every modern convenience.

Goldener Krone
Linzergasse 48; tel: 0662-872 300; www.hotel-goldenekrone. com; €; bus: 4; map p.132 C4

It might be advisable to ask for a back room away from the street noise, but this family-run hotel offers great hospitality and a convenient central location for affordable prices.

Hotel Amadeus
Linzergasse 43–5; tel: 0662-871 401; www.hotelamadeus.at; €; bus: 4; map p.133 C4

Perhaps the best value three-star hotel in the city, the misleadingly narrow corridors of the Amadeus give on to rooms decorated in a variety of delightful individual styles, with the possibility of being blessed with a four-poster bed. Rooms at the back of the building – itself 500 years old and under a preservation order – have views of the St Sebastian cemetery. Staff are

helpful and the location is highly convenient.

Hotel Bergland
Rupertgasse 15; tel: 0662-872 318; www.berglandhotel.at; €; map p.133 D4

This low-budget hotel has accommodating staff and a wide price range, from en suites through to rooms with shared bathroom for the cash-strapped traveller.

Hotel Bristol
Makartplatz 4; tel: 0662-873 557; www.bristol-salzburg.at; €€€; bus: 1, 2, 3, 5, 6, 25, 840; map p.132 C3

Housed in a fine *fin-de-siècle* building, conveniently close to Mozart's house and the Schloss Mirabell, this is one of the most charming and luxurious of the city's high-range hotels, extravagantly furnished from its penthouse rooms down to the restaurants and piano bar.

Hotel Gablerbräu
Linzergasse 9; tel: 0662-889 65; www.centralhotel.at; €; bus: 4; map p.132 C3

Located within the walls of a renovated 15th century guesthouse, this hotel boasts spacious rooms, substantial breakfasts and complimentary prosecco on arrival. The bar has a cellar-like feel and is decorated with photographs of jazz greats; the restaurant is very popular with locals.

Hotel Mozart
Franz-Josef-Strasse 27; tel: 0662-872 274; www.hotel-mozart.at; €; bus: 21, 22; map p.133 C4

The Mozart is a comfortable mid-range hotel a short walk out of the new town. Its creamy décor, with flower murals in the stairwells, is cosy rather than bland and the staff excel even among the attentive and hospitality-conscious Salzburgers. Bathrooms are small, but

Prices for a double room including breakfast in low season:
€€€ over €220
€€ €150–€220
€ up to €150

boast bathtubs as well as showers.

Hotel Sacher

Schwarzstrasse 5–7; tel: 0662-889 770; www.sacher.com; €€€; bus: 27; map p.132 C3

Founded in 1866, this riverside hotel is renowned for impeccable service at the highest level and a vast range of facilities including steam room and sauna as well as a gym and a variety of venues for top-class cuisine and refreshment. The building itself is the work of architect Carl Freiherr von Schwarz.

Hotel Sheraton

Auerspergstrasse 4; 0662-889 990; www.starwoodhotels.com; €€; bus: 22; map p.132 B4

With an appealing restaurant and a beautiful location right on the fringe of the Mirabellgarten, this is a hotel jockeying for top place with the other high-end establishments of the city centre.

Hotel Stadtkrug

Linzergasse 20; tel: 0662-873 5450; www.stadtkrug.at; €; bus: 4; map p.132 C3

The autographs on the walls attest to the popularity of this hotel with those who come to perform at the Festival. The hotel has the added bonus of a roof garden from which one can overlook the city.

NH Salzburg-City

Franz-Josef-Strasse 26; tel: 0662-882 0410; www.nh-hotels.com; €; bus: 21, 22; map p.133 C4

The City is a modern chain hotel whose principal attractions are the reliability of serv-ice and proximity to New Town attractions like the Mirabell.

Pension Arenberg

Blumensteinstrasse 8; tel: 0662-640 097; www.arenberg-salzburg.at; €; bus: 6, 7, 20; map p.133 E3

On the slopes of the Kapuzinerberg, the hotel offers a quiet retreat from the city, with the personal touch of the Leopacher family who pride themselves on traditional host-ing. The 13 spacious rooms are decorated in soft hues and all have a balcony. An attractive garden and cheerful breakfast room (no restaurant).

Pension Elisabeth

Vogelweiderstrasse 52; tel: 0662-871 664; www.pension-elisabeth.at; €; bus: 2

With 14 basic rooms and a charm of its own, this is a great place for budget trav-ellers who still like a touch of elegance. A very bright, clean establishment. Some rooms have shared bathrooms, and there is one apartment.

St Sebastian

Linzergasse 41; tel: 0662-871 386; www.st-sebastian-salzburg.at; €; bus: 4; map p.133 C4

Although popularity in high season means reservations are essential, it is worth the effort for travellers on a budget to stay at the St Sebastian, which boasts laundry facilities and shared kitchens for its guests.

Stein Hotel

Giselakai 3–5; tel: 0662-874 3460; www.hotelstein.at; €; bus: 3, 5, 6, 7, 8; map p.132 C3

Directly on the Salzach River, the newly renovated (and now a designer) hotel has been in operation since 1399. The rooms are modern and stylish, the grander ones with marble bathrooms, and those at the front have a superb view over the Altstadt. At the top of the hotel is the famous **Steinterrace Café** with commanding views over the old city and a DJ on Friday and Saturday.

SEE ALSO CAFÉS AND BARS, P.40

Around Salzburg

Astoria Hotel

Maxglaner Hauptstrasse 7; tel: 0662-834 277; www.salzburg astoria.com; €; bus 27; map p.134 C3

A 15-min walk from the city centre, the Astoria is tasteful and unpretentious. A 20th-century hotel, renovated in 2001 and reopened under new, family management. Much of the décor features modern art. Some rooms have

Above: a chic bathroom in the Arthotel Blaue Gans, *see p.80.*

a winter garden balcony. No restaurant but a delightful coffee-shop selling home-made cakes and other sweet treats.

Doktorschössl
Glaserstrasse 7–10; tel: 0662-623 088; www.doktorschloessl.com; €; bus: 7; map p.135 C3
An attractive house dating from 1670, when it was home to Dr Franz Mayr, physician to Prince Archbishop Wolf Dietrich von Raitenau and son-in-law of Santino Solari, the builder of Salzburg Cathedral. Most of the spacious rooms have views of the Gaisberg or the Untersberg. There is an outdoor pool, pleasant garden, and a bar and restaurant in a vaulted hall.

Gästehaus Scheck
Rennbahnstrasse 11; tel: 0662-623 268; www.hotel-scheck.com; €; bus: 6, 7, 20; map p.133 E2
A family-run hotel in the

attractive suburb of Aigen, east of the city, set in a lovely garden. It feels as though you are in the country, but the town centre is only a 20-minute walk away, along the banks of the Salzach River. The rooms have clean white walls and attractive wooden period furniture. No restaurant, but breakfast is provided.

Haus Am Moos
Moosstrasse 186a; tel: 0662-824 921; www.ammoos.at; €; bus: 21
A lovely private house in the semi-rural area of Moosstrasse at the foot of the Untersberg. Close to the countryside and only a 15-minute bus ride into town. It is all about the family Strassers' personal touch. High-standard rooms, all with private bathroom, and a picture-perfect garden with large pool. Breakfast is included.

Haus Steiner
Moosstrasse 156c; tel: 0662-830 031; www.haussteiner.com; €; bus: 21
A beautiful Alpine-style house surrounded by countryside, but only a 15-minute bus ride from the centre of town.

Family-run, traditional Austrian hospitality. Spacious rooms with fine views; some have balconies. It has a cheerful breakfast room.

Hotel Friesacher
Hellbrunnerstrasse 17; Anif; tel: 06246-8977; www.hotelfriesacher.com; €€; bus: 25; map p.135 C3
Set just outside the city, close to Hellbrunn, with a quick bus ride into the city centre. The comfortable rooms are well-decorated in a traditional style, but even more attractive is the attached spa with a lovely outdoor pool. Excellent service and a decent restaurant make this a great alternative to staying in the busy city centre.

Hallein and Berchtesgaden

BERCHTESGADEN
Hotel zum Türken
83471 Obersalzberg; tel: 08652-2428; www.hotel-zum-tuerken.com; €; map p.134 C1
This characterful old pension, opened in 1911, has an interesting history, including being used by the Gestapo during World War II; and not many hotels have their own air-raid

Prices for a double room including breakfast in low season:
€€€ over €220
€€ €150–€220
€ up to €150

shelter. In a great location with wonderful views it has large comfortable rooms.

InterContinental Resort Berchtesgaden

Hintereck 1, Berchtesgaden; tel: 08652-975 50; www.intercontinental.com; €€; map p.134 C1

Controversial when it opened as due to its history some felt that Berchtesgaden should not be promoted as a tourist resort, this hotel has nonetheless won visitors over by its excellent facilities and wonderful location amid the Bavarian Alps. The complex and spa is well-designed and the outdoor heated pool has great views.

HALLEIN
Schloss Haunsperg

Hammerstrasse 51, Oberalm bei Hallein; tel: 06245-806 62; www.schlosshaunsperg.com; €–€€; map p.135 C2

Run by the von Gernerth-Mautner Markhof family, this castle is a wonderful place to stay, with its own Baroque chapel, huge grounds and palatial rooms. For all its grandeur it is not at all toffee-nosed and very family-friendly. The rates are low for a touch of aristocratic living.

The Salzkammergut

BAD ISCHL
Goldener Ochs

Grazer Strasse 4; tel: 06132-235 290; www.goldenerochs.at; €–€€; map p.137 D2

An attractive four-star establishment in a pretty imperial yellow building with rearward facing balconies. The Schweiger family offer fine service in this hotel, which includes a courtyard restaurant and indoor swimming pool.

Goldenes Schiff

Adalbert-Stifter-Kai 3; tel: 06132-24 241; www.goldenes-schiff.at; €; map p.137 D2

Take a balcony room with a view over the water for the best stay in this modern but pleasant and well-appointed riverside establishment.

Hubertushof

Götzstrasse 1; tel: 06132-24 445; www.hubertushof.co.at; €; map p.137 D2

Traditional values are to the fore at this hotel, run by the Panhuber family with an exceptional level of hospitality. There is a small pool and sauna, good breakfasts are served and the restaurant is a popular Bad Ischl venue offering a traditional menu.

GMUNDEN
Hotel Freistiz Roith

Traunsteinstrasse 87; tel: 07612-64905; www.schlosshotel.at; €€; map p.137 E3

This 'Schloss Hotel' is within a 17th-century castle, a short walk out of town but exchanging city-centre convenience for an absorbing lakeside ambiance. Guests can enjoy the views from balconies or the extensive terrace. Includes small-scale spa facilities.

Hotel Schwan

Rathausplatz 8; tel: 07612-63 391; www.seehotel-schwan.at; €; map p.137 E3

With every room boasting a balcony view of the lake and fresh lake fish being served in the dining room below, the Schwan on the main square is one of the town's most appealing, as well as conveniently situated, establishments.

ELSEWHERE
Hotel Winzer

Kogl 66, St Georgen im Attergau; tel: 07667-6387; www.hotel-winzer.at; €; map p.137 D3

This excellent-value hotel is renowned for its spa. Attrac-

Below: the Hotel Sacher on the banks of the Salzach, *see p.83.*

tive décor and attentive service are complemented by a range of fitness classes and de-stressing facilities.
SEE ALSO SPAS, P.119

Pension Falkensteiner
Salzburgerstrasse 11, St Gilgen; tel: 06227-2395; www.pension-falkensteiner.at; €; map p.135 E3
An attractive place run by the family owners. As well as possessing its own garden, the hotel's other major draw is bicycle hire; the perfect way to explore the Wolfgangsee at your own pace.

Schloss Fuschl
Schloss Strasse 19, Hof bei Salzburg; tel: 6229-225 30; www.schlossfuschlsalzburg. com; €€€; map p.136 C2
Betwen Salzburg and the Salzkammergut on a peninsula jutting out into a lake, this castle-hotel is in a lovely location and is ideally placed for exploring both the city and the neighbouring region. Opulent and luxurious, if you have the money this is a place to really spoil yourself. If you fancy a bit of local colour you can stay in the nearby Jägerhaus (www.sheratonfuschlseesalzburg.

com), decorated like a Salzkammergut hunting lodge. If that conjures up visions of Mitteleuropa kitsch, here it is done beautifully and with restraint.

Schloss Mondsee
Schlosshof 1a, Mondsee; tel: 06232-5001; www.schloss mondsee.at; €€; map p.135 E4
This lovely spa hotel has stylish minimalist rooms (lots of stripped wood) set in a large castle. Apart from the good restaurants, the main attraction, however, is the spa itself which has excellent facilities.
SEE ALSO SPAS, P.119

Seegasthof Lackner
Mondseestrasse 1, Mondsee; tel: 06232-23590; www.seehotel-lackner.at; €; map p.135 E4
Make the most of the resort lifestyle and head for the Seegasthof Lackner, an attractive lakeside establishment perfect for families, and even able to furnish sailing craft for its residents.

Hallstatt and Dachstein

Gasthof Hallberg
Seestrasse 113; tel: 06134-8709; www.pension-hallberg.at.tf; €; map p.137 D1

In Hallstatt, the Gasthof Hallberg offers a pleasingly eccentric guest-house experience, its communal areas decorated with unusual finds from the lake's depths and its rooms offering some great views of both the lake and the surrounding mountains.

Gasthof Höllwirt
Obertraun 29; tel: 06131-394; www.hoellwirt.at; €; map p.137 D1
For those who choose to spend a night close to the famous ice caves, this offers a traditional Austrian guest-house experience in the district of the Hallstätter See and Dachstein mountains; the restaurant offers typical dishes of the region, including fish from the lakes.

The Lammertal and Lungau

Schloss Moosham
Moosham 12, Unternberg; tel: 06476-305; www.schloss-moosham.info; €; map p.139 E2
The owners of the castle has some delightful holiday appartments to rent in an old farm building nearby (some have views of the castle). The

---

Below: the interior of Schloss Fuschl.

Above: Kurhotel Mirabell, Bad Gastein.

rooms which are excellent value, are clean and attractive, and panelled with wood.

The Salzach and High Tauern

BAD GASTEIN

All the hotels below offer spa treatments.

SEE ALSO SPAS, P.119

Grand Park Hotel
Kurgartenstrasse 26, Bad Hofgastein; tel: 06432-63 560; www.grandparkhotel.at; €–€€; map p.138 C3
Further down the valley in Bad Hofgastein, this large luxury hotel has all you could want for a spa break. Large comfortable rooms and excellent health and beauty amenities at a good price.

Hoteldorf Grüner Baum
Kötschachtal 25, Bad Gastein; tel: 06434-25 160; www.hoteldorf.com; €€–€€€; map p.138 C2
This hotel offers much more than treatments. In a beautiful location with very comfortable rooms and excellent service. Do not miss a visit to the 'healing caves' nearby (www.gasteiner-heilstollen.com).

Hotel Salzburger Hof
Grillparzerstrasse 1, Bad Gastein; tel: 06434-20370; www.salzburgerhof.com; €€€; map p.138 C2
A grand old hotel that first opened in 1907 to cater for the royalty and heads of state that flocked to the valley for the cures. Comfortable without being over-the-top.

Kurhotel Mirabell
Bismarckstrasse 4–8, Bad Gastein; tel: 06434-3301; www.kurhotel-mirabell.at; €€; map p.138 C2
A comfortable, if very traditional 'cure hotel' – rather charming in its own way – that is largely dedicated to sorting out medical problems.

ST JOHANN AND GOLDEGG

Der Seehof
Hofmark 8, Goldegg am See; tel: 06415-813 70; www.derseehof.at; €; map p.138 C3
This family-run design hotel is set in a traditional house by the lake. The beautifully decorated rooms, at bargain prices, are all given individual themes and the

hotel is family-friendly. They even run cooking courses.

Hotel Brückenwirt
Hauptstrasse 78, St Johann im Pongaul; tel: 06412-425 90; www.hotel-brueckenwirt.at; €; map p.138 C4
Attractive, central hotel that has been open for 150 years. The rooms are modern and light with tasteful traditional touches. The restaurant is known for its good local food.

ZELL AM SEE

Hotel Lebzelter
Dreifaltigkeitsstrasse 7; tel: 06542-7760; www.hotel-lebzelter.at; €; map p.138 B3
A large, attractive hotel in the town centre. The rooms are modern and clean and guests have free access to the nearby public swimming pool.

Mavida
Kirchenweg 11; tel: 06542-5410; www.mavida.at; €€; map p.138 B3
This design and spa hotel is definitely the classiest place to stay in Zell am See. Wonderfully chic, everything is beautifully laid out and the spa facilities are second to none. Wood fires in the rooms during winter add a nice romantic touch. Highly recommended.

Salzburgerhof
Auerspergstrasse 11; tel: 06542-765; www.salzburgerhof.at; €€€; map p.138 B3
This excellent luxury spa-resort is nestled in the mountains. Friendly and well-run, it is especially good for active travellers due to its location, providing bicycles with which to explore the local area.

Prices for a double room including breakfast in low season:
€€€ over €220
€€ €150–€220
€ up to €150

87

Language

The official language of Austria is German, but the legacies of European empires and nation-building mean that this small country is favoured with a wide variety of dialects and accents which are highly distinctive, even to keen-eared non-German speakers. The varieties of Austrian German have strong ties to regional identities, with the borders of the nation's federal states strongly demarcating language variation. With Austria having acceded to the European Union in 1995, its variety of the German language received protected status within Europe. *See also Food and Drink p.76–7* for a guide to food vocabulary.

Rückga Shop, A

return shop, e

Salzburg's Dialect

Salzburgers speak a form of the Austro-Bavarian dialect which, as its name suggests, stretches across the border with Germany to Munich and beyond. That said, Bavarian speech is notably distinct from its Salzburg sister in its rhythms and pronunciation.

Originating among Germanic tribes occupying what is now Bavaria and western Austria, the Austro-Bavarian language spread along the Danube in the era of Charlemagne's Frankish empire, during which period Salzburg's archbishopric was first established.

While the prestige language used in mass media and which is the medium education tends towards Hochdeutsch, or High German, Salzburgers use the Austro-Bavarian dialect in everyday life. Most Austrians speak very good English, and will switch from dialect to Hochdeutsch where necessary, but even so, foreign visitors with quite a high standard of German may find themselves occasionally

The nature and history of population movement in Central Europe, so long the stomping ground of trans-national empires, means that the Austro-Bavarian dialect is also spoken in its various forms by communities running to hundreds of thousands in the Czech Republic, Germany, Hungary and Italy.

wrongfooted by the linguistic differences. Nonetheless, any attempt to speak Austrian German is much appreciated and even non-linguists can show their respect and good will by offering a traditional Austrian greeting of *Grüss Gott* when encountering native speakers.

False Friends

Just because it sounds like English does not mean it is. *Ich bekomme ein Baby*, for example, does not mean 'I am becoming a baby', but 'I am having a baby'; *ein Berliner* is a jam doughnut and *also* does not mean 'also', but usually 'so' or 'therefore'. Some loan words

can be very confusing, too. *Aktuell* means 'up-to-date' or 'fashionable', not 'actual', and *Ich komme eventuell* could mean that 'I am not coming at all'. A good translation would be 'I might come'. *Ein Knicker* is a scrooge and *ein Schellfish* is a haddock.

Pronunciation Guide

a short 'a' or long 'ah'
ei long 'i' as in 'isolation'
e long 'ay' or short 'eh'
ie 'ee'
ö 'er'
eu and äu 'oy'
u 'oo'
au 'ow'
ü 'euw'
u short 'u' as in 'put'

Useful Words and Phrases

Hello *Grüss Gott/Servus*
Good morning *Guten morgen*
Good afternoon *Guten nachmittag*
Good evening *Guten abend*
Good night *Gute nacht*
Do you speak English? *Spechen sie Englisch?*
I don't understand *Ich verstehe nicht*

e Audioguide
sgang
ıdioguide
t

Left: clear signs at a Salzburg museum.

Although standard German in Austria does differ from that of its sister nation to the west in a number of fields, including legal and technical language, cooking is the topic in which the distinctions are most noticeable. For example, tomatoes here are not mundane *Tomaten* but heavenly *Paradeiser*; German *Pfannkuchen* (pancakes) are *Palatschinken* in Austria; and the potatoes known to a German as *Kartoffeln* are the *Erdapfel* (earth apple) of the Austrian's eye.

Yes *Ja*
No *Nein*
Excuse me *Entschluldigen Sie, bitte*
Please *Bitte*
Thank you *Danke*
What time is it? *Wie spät ist es?*
Nine o'clock *Neun Uhr*
Half past nine *Halb zehn*
Today *Heute*
Tomorrow *Morgen*
Yesterday *Gestern*
Castle/palace *Burg/Schoss*
Church *Kirche*
Cathedral *Dom*
Museum *Museum*
Tower *Turm*
Town hall *Rathaus*
Town square *Stadtplatz*
Station *Bahnhof*
Airport *Flughafen*
Harbour *Hafen*
How do I get to…? *Wie komme ich am besten zu…?*

Left *Links*
Right *Rechts*
Straight on *Geradeaus*
Opposite *Gegenüber*
Help! *Hilfe!*
Single room *Einzelzimmer*
Double room *Doppelzimmer*
With bath/shower *Mit Bad/ Dusche*

Numbers

0 *null*
1 *eins*
2 *zwei*
3 *drei*
4 *vier*
5 *fünf*
6 *sechs*
7 *sieben*
8 *acht*
9 *neun*
10 *zehn*
11 *elf*
12 *zwölf*
13 *dreizehn*

20 *zwanzig*
21 *einundzwanzig*
30 *dreissig*
40 *vierzig*
50 *fünfzig*
100 *hundert*

Slang

a right mess *eine Schweinerei*
bastard *Arschloch, du blöde Kuh, du Schweinehund*
bloody hell! *verdammt noch mal!*
great, magic *klasse, super, toll, Spitze, leiwand*
oh my God! *du lieber Gott!*
pissed *besoffen, fett, voll*
pissed off *sauer, grantig, angefressen*
shit *Scheisse, Mist*
stupid *doof, blöd, deppert, narrisch*
wow! *Mensch! Mah! Wahnsinn!*

Below: 'Lean back with your feet slightly raised. Warning! Do not attempt to brake! At the bottom move off the slide immediately!'

Zurücklehnen - Beine leicht anheben
Achtung: Nicht bremsen!
Nach dem Rutschen sofort wegtreten!

Literature and Theatre

ider nicht mehr sprechen weil
I'm afraid I can't speak any

Skizzenbuch, 1976

I n addition to serving as the setting for literary
works, Salzburg has been home to a number
of significant writers, especially since the turn of
the 19th century, including Stefan Zweig,
Thomas Bernhard and Hugo von Hofmannsthal.
As well as being an important centre for
German-language theatre – in part due to the
festival started by Hofmannsthal and Max
Reinhard – it is also the location of the charming
Salzburger Marionettentheater that is a great
experience for adults and children alike.

nerung,
er Träume

ms

Beate: I
„Du sch

Beate:
"Don't

Skizzenb

Stefan Zweig

Among the most famous
writers to have lived in the
city is Stefan Zweig
(1882–1942). A biographer,
essayist and novelist, Zweig
dwelt at No. 5, Kapuzinerberg from 1919 to 1938,
when he went into exile in
England and then Brazil.
Although Vienna-born, Zweig
produced much of his work
while a Salzburg resident.

His historical biographies
were particularly significant
as texts which served to dis-
cuss contemporary anxieties
through the prism of the represented past, although
today in the English-speaking
world, his most famous work
is *Die Welt von Gestern* ('The
World of Yesterday').

During the inter-war years,
Zweig sought to preserve a
pacifist and humanist culture
which he saw as threatened
by the decline of the Austro-
Hungarian Empire and sub-
sequent rise of anti-Semitism
and ultimately Nazism.

Zweig's parents were both
Jewish and the writer saw
himself as merely an 'acci-
dental Jew', fully assimilated

Above: Zweig with his wife Lotte Altmann in Brazil
at the end of their lives.

into European humanist culture until the rise of racial
persecution in his homeland.

The World of Yesterday
pays tribute to that culture
through autobiography and
cultural analysis, but it bears
the tone of a swan song and
in 1942, Zweig and his wife
Lotte chose to commit joint
suicide with an overdose
rather than witness what they
expected to be a future world
without intellectual or personal freedom.

SEE ALSO THE NEW TOWN, P.11

Aharon Appelfeld

Aharon Appelfeld was born in
1932, in Bukovina (now part
of the Ukraine) rather than
Austria, and has been a resident of Israel for more than
half a century, but his 1980
work *Badenheim ir Nofesh*
(translated as Badenheim
1939) provides an important
perspective on the superfi-
cially placid and charming
ambiance of today's
Salzburger Land.

The novel chronicles the
gradual persecution of the

Michael P. Steinberg

American researcher Michael P. Steinberg has also treated this theme, providing a readable, although academic, analysis of this opposition in his *Austria as Theatre and Ideology: The Meaning of the Salzburg Festival*. This book traces, from the festival's inception to its 1999 celebration, the production and exploitation of a controlled image of Catholic, Germanic Austria for the purposes of bolstering national identity.

Thomas Berhard

Another writer deeply involved in discussion of contemporary Austrian identity was Thomas Bernhard (1931–1989), a Salzburg figure whose poetry, plays and semi-autobiographical prose fiction offer a bleak and withdrawn, but compelling view of the world. A typical Bernhard diagnosis of reality appears in his work *Gathering Evidence*, when he offers this account of Salzburg: 'This city of my fathers is in reality a terminal disease

Among Zweig's more available works of fiction is the 1941 novella *Schachnovelle* (translated as 'Chess Story' or 'The Royal Game'), which deals with a man's obsession with chess in the light of Nazi persecution. Zweig's most famous biography was *Erasmus of Rotterdam* which, continuing Zweig's concern with the endurance of humanist culture, he saw as a 'concealed autobiography'.

Jewish residents and tourists within the fictional Austrian spa town of the title. Officials from the mysterious Sanitation Department begin inspections of the town and its people. Staple leisure activities in the countryside and musical practice for a forthcoming festival give way to an enforced gaiety limited to a hotel, swimming pool and pastry shop. Gradually the town is shut off from the outside world and transmutes into a ghetto from which the internees can only guess at their final fate.

By superimposing the images of tourist Austria and the Nazi persecution, Appelfeld dramatises the extent to which Salzburg and similar towns are involved in Austria's ongoing discomfort in acknowledging the painful history of its Jewish population. The city has historically figured in conservative eyes as the 'true Austria', conservative, Catholic and heartily rural as opposed to a supposedly impure Vienna of urban decadence, immigration, intellectualism and above all Jewishness.

Below: Aharon Appelfeld

Above: Max Reinhardt and Hugo von Hofmannsthal, co-founders of the Salzburg Festival.

which its inhabitants acquire through heredity or contagion…Anyone who is familiar with the city knows it to be a cemetery of fantasy and desire, beautiful on the surface but horrifying underneath.'

Bernhard was initially a student of performance at the city's Mozarteum, but attacks of tuberculosis requiring long sanatorium stays left him increasingly introspective and repelled by the social world of mid-20th century Austria.

Working in a grocer's store in a neglected district of the city opened his eyes to the lives of Salzburg's marginalised, impoverished and dispossessed citizens.

Inspired by a grandfather who had been a writer, Bernhard moved first into journalism and then into the lifelong production of a body of work which won him great renown in the German-speaking world and beyond.

Bernhard's writing resists the pastoral vision of Austria offered from the time of the Habsburgs through to *The Sound of Music* and beyond, emphasising rather mendacity, stupidity and the oppression

he attributes to the Catholic church and Austrian government. Bernhard's intense style and relentless pessimism make him an exhausting writer, but as he pointed out, his world 'was indeed a cesspit, but one which engendered the most intricate and beautiful forms if one looked into it long enough.'

Bernhard's prose style was highly challenging, based as it was on pushing the German language beyond conventional bounds, and his work took some time to reach English-speaking readers. Even now, with most of his prose works available, Bernhard's plays and poetry remain difficult to obtain in translation, and his general literary reputation lags behind the esteem in which he is held even by French and Spanish readers.

Hugo von Hofmannsthal

Hugo von Hofmannsthal, an earlier Austrian writer, had bridged the worlds of theatre and literature much as Bernhard did; but while Bernhard's misanthropic works articulated a harsh criticism of one vision of Austria, Hofmannsthal's

contribution to Salzburg's cultural life, a 1911 adaptation of the English morality play *Everyman*, was intended to bolster a version of Austrian national identity.

While Hofmannsthal was essentially a Viennese writer, and prose works like 'Ein Brief' (translated as 'The Chandos Letter') reflect the concerns of Vienna at the *fin de siècle*, he was also a co-founder of the Salzburg Festival, to which perhaps his most important contribution as a writer was the adapted *Jedermann* that remains a centrepiece of the event to this day.

Hofmannsthal drew on the common European heritage in works like *The Salzburg Great Theatre* of the World, adapted from Spain's Renaissance dramatist Calderón de la Barca, seeing his work as playwright, translator and impresario as the best means for a

liberal humanist artist to intervene against the rise of extremist politics, 'helping [the German-speaking] people to find their way back to a true spiritual expression.'
SEE ALSO FESTIVALS, P.68

Theatre

While there is a long and important tradition of drama in Salzburg, contemporary theatre in the city tends to be in German, and English-language productions are rare. The Salzburger Landestheater is one of the most prestigious of such institutions in Austria, with two stages offering a variety of classic and contemporary drama, while alternative offerings tend to appear at ARGE Kultur. Another drama venue, the world-famous Marionettentheater, tends to focus on opera and musicals in its puppet shows, but is an awe-inspiring experience for people of all ages.

ARGEkultur Salzburg
Josef-Preis-Allee 16, 5020 Salzburg; tel: 0662-848 784; www.argekultur.at; map p.133 D2
Drama performances occasionally take place at Salzburg's latest modern arts venue.

The Landestheater
Schwarzstrasse 22, 5020 Salzburg; tel: 0662-87151 2222; www.salzburger-landestheater.at; map p.132 B3
The Salzburger Landestheater, the city's main venue for serious drama (predominantly in German), as well as some opera and ballet, was built in 1892–3 and was reconstructed in 1938. Behind the Landestheater building is the Studio Theatre and the Puppet Theatre.

Salzburger Marionettentheater
Schwarzstrasse 24; tel: 0662-872 406; www.marionetten.at; bus; map p.132 B3
Abridged versions of famous

Johann Peter Hilverding brought the tradition of puppetry to the Salzburg court in 1673, though it was his son who began introducing elements of the *Commedia dell'arte* to his shows. The pioneer of modern Salzburg puppetry, Professor Anton Aicher, made his debut with Mozart's *Bastien and Bastienne* on 27 February 1913 and the theatre has never looked back.

works, from Shakespeare to Mozart, running to no more than an hour, together with a sympathetic attitude from the staff, mean that even the youngest and most fidgety can experience the incredible *mise en scene* and choreography on offer here. The programme is heavily dependent on the current repertoire and always subject to change, but the one-hour performances (an abridged *Magic Flute* and a Mozart 'best of' compilation) usually take place at 2pm and 4pm. The theatre is open year-round but the players do sometimes tour, as in November 2007 when they took a puppet *Sound of Music* to the United States.
SEE ALSO CHILDREN, P.54

Bookshop
Buchhandlung Höllrigl
Sigmund-Haffner-Gasse 10; tel: 0662 841 146; Mon–Fri 9am–6pm, Sat 9am–5pm; map p.132 C3
A very central bookshop with a large range of German-language literature as well as reference works. There is also a small section of Enligsh-language books.

Left: Thomas Bernhard's *Ein Fest für Boris* at the 2007 Salzburg Festival.

93

Monuments

In a place as devoted to its own history as Salzburg, monuments are vital markers of the past and our relationship to it, focal points crafted to commemorate and perpetuate the various competing legacies of the region. As one monumental artist put it recently, 'Anybody who sits and thinks long enough can connect with invisible forces.' So much of Salzburg's charm is drawn from these invisible historical influences, with Mozart taking pride of place; contemplation of its local monuments only intensifies our appreciation of this unique corner of Austria's past and present.

Above: Mozart stands proud on Mozartplatz.

Above: the Mozart family grave.

Salzburg

Mozart Memorials

Unsurprisingly, the figure of Mozart plays a central role in the memorial culture of present-day Salzburg. Monuments were augured well in the region from the day in 1841 when workers, preparing to install the statue of the composer at the **Mozartplatz** (map p.133 C3), found a slab from a marble floor bearing an inscription dedicating that spot only to happiness and never misery. That said, this good omen almost immediately bore witness to the conflicts and controversies typical of people disputing remembrance of the past: when Mozart's statue was finally unveiled, having missed the 50th anniversary of his death by a year, Mozart's son exploited the ceremony as an attempt to promote his own standing as a composer and performer, only to be driven off stage as he launched into a recital of his own works.

The statue is considered to be a poor likeness and even anachronistic, showing as it does Mozart with a pencil rather than the quill pens which were common in his time. A more recent Mozart sculpture also courted controversy when, in 2006, a painted bronze nude of the composer produced by Markus Lupertz was vandalised by disapproving locals.

A far more radical approach to memorialising Mozart exists in Marina Abramovic's 2004 installation ***The Spirit of Mozart*** (Schwarzstrasse and Ledergasse, map p.132 C2), located on the riverside walk of the Schwarzstrasse near Café Bazar. The artist has installed eight metal chairs where one is supposed to 'sit, close one's

Left: the wonderful Baroque Residenz Fountain.

Baroque fountains, each of which has a connection with horses. On Residenzplatz, Altstadt's largest square, is the **Residenz Fountain** (map p.132 C3) with its rearing horses spouting water, created by Tommaso di Garona between 1656 and 1661. The fountain is 15m high and is said to be the largest Baroque fountain outside Italy. If you are visiting in wintertime, though, you will find it covered up for protection against the elements.

Close by, on Kapitelplatz, is **Neptune's Fountain** (map p.132 C2), built in 1732 by the sculptor Anton Pfaffinger on the site of one of the horse ponds during the rule of Archbishop Leopold Anton Firmian.

Further west, on Herbert-von-Karajan-Platz is the attractive **Pferde-schwemme** (Horse Trough and Fountain, map p.132 B3), which incorporates a stunning mural of horses. The fountain was built in 1695 by

Mozart is not the only composer whose legacy is honoured in the region. In the town square of Gmunden the Franz Schubert memorial – a bust facing out over the Traunsee – recalls the composer's 1825 trip through the region with Johann Michael Vogl. They stayed at a building on the Theatergasse, marked today by a memorial plaque.

The Altstadt
A.E.I.O.U.
Max-Reinhardt-platz; map p.132 B3
Anselm Kiefer's artwork *A.E.I.O.U.*, was commissioned as part of the same series as Abramovic's Mozart installation. *A.E.I.O.U.* is a small, squat hut, within which is displayed a painting *Awake in the Gypsy Camp* and a display of books apparently spewing thorn branches. The installation is named for a Habsburg motto *Austria Est Imperare Orbi Universo* – 'Austria is to rule the whole world' – and also cites from major 20th-century poet Ingeborg Bachmann: 'Awake in the gypsy camp and awake in the desert tent, the sand runs out of our hair, your age and mine and the age of the world are not measured in years.' This deliberately provocative allusion to the nomadic lifestyle challenges viewers to reimagine the imperial ambitions of the past and look towards a better future.
Fountains
The Altstadt of Salzburg is home to three lovely

eyes, forget oneself, lose all sense of time' and reconcile oneself with the bustle of the traffic, the murmur of the River Salzach and the incessant trill of the pigeons. Surprisingly effective, especially in spring and summer when the chairs are warmed by the sun, *The Spirit of Mozart* is meant to evoke the composer's troubled relationship with his home city and inspire a new reconciliation. A welcome alternative to the surfeit of *Mozartkugeln*. As Abramovic herself puts it: 'I would like to create a place of meditation in Salzburg, where people can rise above the surrounding mountain face.'

Below: the Pferdeschwemm.

Right: the chapel at Oberndorf has this stained-glass window commemorating Franz Gruber, composer of *Silent Night*.

Bernard Michael Mandl to serve as the washing area for the prince archbishops' horses that were kept in stables next door. This adjacent site along Hofstallgasse has subsequently been converted into the **Festspielhäuser** (map p.132 B3). Originally the fountain used to face the stables but in a remodelling in 1732 it was turned 90 degrees.

St Peter's Cemetery
Festungsgasse; map p.132 C2

The cemetery behind St Peter's Monastery is the elegant, even romantic, resting place of Salzburg's noblest families. It is located at the base of the Mönchsberg and is the oldest cemetery in Salzburg still in use. The present layout of the churchyard dates from 1627 and, on first impression, the burial plots seem haphazardly laid out. Most of the graves have markers which have an enamel centrepiece painted with rich colours.

Many of these have a lamp dangling from the post supporting the elaborate design. In the centre of the graveyard lies St Margaret's Chapel which holds the remains of Mozart's sister, Nannerl, and the famous musician Michael Haydn.

The Wildermann
Wilhelm Furtängler Garten, map p.132 B3

Between the Festspielhäuser and the back of the Kollegienkirche is a little patch of grass that is the Wilhelm Furtwängler Garten. Guarding the entrance to this is a depiction of the Green Man, standing over the **Wild Man of the Fish Fountain**, the statue of whom dates back to 1620.

The New Town
Mirabell Gardens
map p.132 B4

Across the river, in the heart of Salzburg among the Mirabell Gardens where the fictional Von Trapp children played, a sombre construction of sand and glass forms the Euthanasia-Aktion memorial, testament to 250 victims of the Nazi hospital regime in 1941. The simple but powerful design recalls the famous Holocaust memorials of Rachel Whiteread; the monument also serves as an acknowledgement of the dark side of Friedrich Ludwig Jahn. This Prussian educator and pioneer of gymnastics is credited with inventing the parallel bars, balance beam and vaulting horse, but his 19th-century nationalist agenda and dedication to physical perfection are also seen as predecessors to the ideology of Nazism.

Around Salzburg

Oberndorf Silent Night Memorial Chapel

map p.136 B3

Almost 200 years ago, in 1818, the first rendition of the famous carol, *Silent Night* was performed in Oberndorf in St Nikolaus Church. Created by Franz Xaver, a schoolmaster and organist, the carol has become one of the most well known and best loved of the festive season. Unfortunately, the original St Nikolaus Church was demolished as Oberndorf was re-located due to the floods in the late 1800s. The memorial chapel, which sits on the site of the original church, was consecrated in 1937 and every year at 5pm on 24 Dec, a memorial service takes place with thousands of people attending. The **Stille Nacht Museum** next to the memorial chapel provides an in depth look into the lives and history of all those involved in the carol.

SEE ALSO MUSEUMS AND GALLERIES, P.101

The Salzkammergut

Bad Ischl

map p.137 D2

At Bad Ischl, the cemetery on Grazer Strasse looks down on the town from a hill and it is here that another composer, Franz Lehár, was buried. A monument has been installed within the colonnade there. Richard Tauber, the tenor who performed many of Lehár's compositions, was to die in exile from the Nazis in 1938, but a plaque on his house on the spa town's Traunkai memorialises his contribution to Austrian opera.

Left: the Pferdeschwemme on Herbert-von-Karajan-Platz.

St Wolfgang

map p.137 D2

In St Wolfgang is the Late Gothic **Pilgrim's Fountain**, cast in 1515 and which stands on the terrace above the market square. The canopy is one of the earliest Renaissance monuments in Austria. Tall gabled houses (some of them several hundred years old) are crowded around the church and the market place.

Hallstatt and Dachstein

Ebensee

map p.137 E2

At Dachstein, a cross on the trails high above the salt mines commemorates Good Friday of 1954, when ten pupils and three teachers from Heilbronn died in a fierce storm on the Dachstein massif. Even more significant markers of loss lie at Ebensee, where the KZ-Friedhof (con-

> In Storbl on the Wolfgangsee, there stands a bust of Emil Jannings, resident of the town and star of silent film who won one of the first ever Oscars and who famously appeared opposite Marlene Dietrich in *The Blue Angel* (see picture, right).

Left: in the gardens of the Kaiservilla in Bad Ischl is this statue of a boy hunting with his dogs.

centration camp cemetery) bears a number of monuments to the tens of thousands who endured forced labour in the tunnels close by. Some have been erected by national and provincial governments, others by the families of the inmates.

Ebensee Camp

Kirchengasse 5; tel: 06133-5601; www.memorial-ebensee.at; Jun–Sept: Tue–Sun 10am–5pm, May–mid-Jun, mid–end Sept: Sat–Sun 10am–5pm; entrance charge

A sister camp to the infamous Mauthausen, where inmates were forced to carry heavy blocks up a vast staircase, Ebensee was used to provide slave labour to dig tunnels secure from Allied bombing raids. Inside the mountain itself, a memorial in English and German offers an account of the camp and its history from foundation to liberation by US forces in 1945.

SEE ALSO MUSEUMS AND GALLERIES, P.102

Museums and Galleries

For such a small city Salzburg has a surprisingly wide spread of museums and galleries, from exhibitions of contemporary art and Old Masters, to the history of the city and the life of Mozart. One of the greatest delights is the Open-air Museum just below the Untersberg, fascinating for both adults and children. The region also has plenty to keep you busy, from memories of the Habsburg Empire in Bad Ischl, to the Celtic past in Hallstatt and Hallein, to the gruesome memories of World War II in Ebensee.

Mönchsberg

Museum der Moderne Salzburg Mönchsberg and Rupertinum
Mönchsberg: Mönchsberg 32; tel: 0662-84222 0403; www.museumdermoderne.at; Tue–Sun 10am–6pm, Wed 10am–9pm, open Mon during Festival; entrance charge; map p.132 B3
Rupertinum: Wiener-Philharmoniker-Gasse 9; tel: 0662-84222 0451; www.museumdermoderne.at; same times as Mönchsberg; entrance charge; map p.132 B3
A lift at Gstättengasse 13 allows access to the top of the Mönchsberg, where you will find the Museum der Moderne. Straight lines, shimmering glass and bright white stone create a stark minimalist edifice, 60m (197ft) above the city. Built on the site of the old Café Winkler (the new museum café, **M32**, is particularly nice), which crowned the plateau for many decades, the new building, designed by Friedrich Hoff Zwink and opened in 2004, respectfully incorporates the old tower into its new structure.

The four levels of bright white Untersberg marble are designed to accommodate an ever-changing and diverse range of exhibitions, plus a permanent collection of works by Klimt, Kokoschka and other, lesser-known artists. Photography is a particularly strong component of the collections and the museum includes the Austrian Gallery of Photography. The glass ceilings and the use of stairways as natural light shafts adds to the viewing pleasure.

The collections were moved to the site on the Mönchsberg from the

Rupertinum building in the Altstadt. This, the original building of the Museum der Moderne, was renovated alongside the construction of the new space on the Mönchsberg and now holds temporary exhbitions of modern and contemporary art.
SEE ALSO CAFÉS AND BARS, P.36

Altstadt

Haus der Natur
Museumsplatz 5; tel: 0662-842 653; www.hausdernatur.at; daily 9am–5pm; entrance charge; map p.132 B3
The Haus der Natur is Salzburg's Natural History Museum. As well as the usual

n der moderne
mönchsberg

Left: a modern sign for a modern museum.

The two main Mozart sites in Salzburg – the house where he was born and the house in which the family subsequently lived – are both administered and owned by the Mozarteum.

On Getreidegasse is the house where he was born on 27 January 1756 and where he lived with his family until 1773. The Mozarts' apartment on the third floor and the rooms on the second floor have been transformed into a museum. On display are manuscripts (facsimiles), documents and souvenirs, and portraits of the family members, including *Mozart at the Piano*, an unfinished 1789 oil painting by Wolfgang's brother-in-law, Joseph Lange. Also here are instruments that were played by the great musician: his concert piano and clavichord, his concert and child's violin, and a viola.

Mozart's Wohnhaus, in the New Town, is housed in the building where the composer and family lived for some 15 years at the end of the 18th century. It is comprised of an attractive, bilingual German/English collection of Mozart memorabilia including manuscripts, first editions,

Left: in the Museum der Moderne Rupertinum.

dead and stuffed specimens, it has an impressive collection of live reptiles and a 36-tank aquarium. Besides wildlife, there are also mineral and geology displays and the Space Research Hall, with a life-size diorama of man's first steps on the moon. The museum is very well laid out and the displays are modern and informative; it also stages a series of changing exhibitions.

Michael Haydn Museum
St-Peter-Hof; tel: 0662-8445 7619; www.concerts-at-five.com; Thur–Tue, May: 10am–noon, July–Sept: 10am–noon, 2–4pm; entrance charge; map p.132 C2
Mozart year in 2006 also coincided with the anniversary of the death of Michael Haydn (1737–1806), composer, brother of the more-famous Joseph Haydn and inhabitant of Salzburg. His life and times are celebrated by this small museum, which has also printed a card giving a 'Michael Haydn Tour' of the

city so you can find the sites associated with this musician. As well as the exhibition the museum also arranges a series of chamber concerts.

Mozart Geburtshaus and Wohnhaus
Geburtshaus: Getreidegasse 9; tel: 0662-844 313; www.mozarteum.at; daily 9am–5.30pm, July–Aug: 9am–8pm; entrance charge; map p.132 B3
Wohnhaus: Makartplatz 8; tel: 0662-8742 2740; www.mozarteum.at; same opening times as the Geburtshaus; entrance charge; map p. 132 C3

Below: Mozart was born here, at Getreidegasse 9.

portraits and musical instruments. The multimedia features, including an audio tour and a cinema showing short education films, are of the first order. In the gift shop, the composer's famous portrait appears reproduced on shelf after shelf bearing every imaginable souvenir from perfume to placemats.

For more serious researchers, the **Ton- und Filmmuseum** (Museum of Film and Sound), housed in the same building, holds an archive of relevant audiovisual material.

Panorama Museum Neue Residenz
Residenzplatz 9; tel: 0662-62080 8730; www.salzburg museum.at; Fri–Wed 9am–5pm, Thur 9am–8pm; entrance charge; map p.132 C3

Enter the museum through the post office on the square. Inside is a large, circular panorama of Salzburg painted in 1829 by Johann Michael Sattler, as well as a small collection of views of the city from the 19th century.

Residenz Galerie
Residenzplatz; tel: 0662-8404 510; http://residenzgalerie.at; Tue–Sun 10am–5pm, open Mon during Festival; entrance charge; map p.132 C3

On the third floor of the Residenz building is the city's art gallery of Old Masters. The small but notable collection contains works by Brueghel, Rembrant and Rubens, as well as some fine 18th-century French paintings by Boucher and Le Brun among others. Naturally there are good holdings of Austrian works, including those by Maulbertsch, Torger and Rottmayr. The gallery also holds temporary exhibitions (see website for details).

Salzburg Museum Neue Residenz
Neue Residenz, Mozartplatz 1; tel: 0662-62080 8700; www.salzburgmuseum.at; Tue–Sun 9am–5pm, Thur 9am–8pm, open Mon 9am–5pm July–Aug, Dec; entrance charge; map p.133 C3

In 2007 the new Salzburg Museum opened in the Neue Residenz on Mozartplatz. Dedicated to the history and conception of the city, it divides the exhibition between two floors: on the first an investigation of the men and women who have shaped it, through ideas, politics and trades; on the second, chronological displays of paintings and artefacts that tell the story of its history. In the basement is a large space given over to temporary exhibitions.

New Town

Salzburg Barockmuseum
Mirabellplatz 3; tel: 0662-877 432; www.barockmuseum.at; Wed–Sun 9am–5pm, Jul–Aug Tue–Sun 10am–5pm; entrance charge; map p.132 B4

The Barockmuseum in the Mirabell Gardens, despite its beautiful setting, tends towards exhibitions of artists' sketches and preliminary works. In terms of actual Baroque art, the museum has less to offer than the various churches and parks of the city and province, and its collection of sketches, while interesting, cannot rival that of Vienna's Albertina.

Around Salzburg

Hangar-7
Wilhelm-Spazier-Strasse 7a; tel: 0662-2197; www.hangar-7.com; daily 9am–10pm; free; bus: 2; map p.134 C3

Completed in 2003, this spectacular building was constructed to house a collection of vintage aircraft. The hangar is a glass and steel dome in the shape of an aircraft wing and is one of the highlights of modern architecture in Salzburg. Situated on the eastern apron of Salzburg's airport, there are two buildings. The first and largest is the hangar that is open to the public. Facing and mirroring it on a smaller scale is Hangar-8, the maintenance hangar.

Salzburger Freilichtmuseum
Hasenweg, Grossgmain; tel: 0662-850 011; www.freilichtmuseum.com; Tue–Sun 9am–6pm, Jul–Aug daily 9am–6pm, last entrance 5pm; entrance charge; bus

Below: Mozart's Gerburtshaus on Getreidegasse, *see p.99.*

Below: sculpture at the Museum der Moderne, *see p.98.*

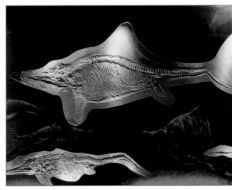

Above: in the Haus der Natur, *see p. 98.*

leaves every hour from Salzburg Hauptbahnhof; map p.136 B3 Tucked beneath the northwest slopes of the Untersberg is the village of Grossgmain, which has an Open-air Museum. The museum is one of the top attractions in the area and has won numerous awards. It includes a collection of old farmhouses that have been transferred from different parts of Salzburg Province and reconstructed with meticulous care. They span the last five centuries, showing how building and farming methods have changed and developed.

There are also many old farm machines to be viewed, and on Sundays and public holidays craftsmen demonstrate the old trades, from woodwork to bee-keeping, shoe-making to beer-brewing. The museum covers an area of 50 hectares (123.5 acres), so you will need a full day to see it all.

Stiegl's Brauwelt
Bräuhausstrasse 9; tel: 0662-8387 1492; www.brauwelt.at; daily 10am–5pm, Jul–Aug 10am–7pm, last entrance 1 hr before closing; entrance charge; bus: 2; map p.134 C3
Attached to the popular local brewery is a museum housing the largest beer

exhibition in the world. Reopened after renovation in 2007, it has a display of brewing techniques, machinery and unusual equipment through the ages. On the tour, you are shown how beer is made from start to finish and can sample the product at the end.

Stille Nacht Museum
Stille-Nacht-Platz 7, Oberndorf; tel: 06272-442 20; www.stillenacht-oberndorf.at; daily Mar–Jan: 9am–4pm; entrance charge; map p.136 B3
Oberndorf's local museum possesses a striking 1520 Gothic altar, the work of G. Guckh, but this is an aside in an institution which has an especially unique focus. The most recorded song in history was first played here in 1818. An exhibition is devoted to 'Silent Night' and its story, from its first performance at St Nikolaus Church across the world. Close by there is even a chapel built in tribute to the song (daily 8am–6pm).

Volkskunde Museum
Monatsschlössl, Hellbrunn; tel: 0662-62080 8500; www.salzburgmuseum.at; daily Apr–Oct: 10am–5.30pm; entrance charge; map p.135 C3
On Hellbrunn Mountain stands the Monatsschlössl

(Month Castle), so-called because it was allegedly built in only one month. It houses a Folklore Museum, which displays costumes, masks, religious artefacts and agricultural equipment from the lively history of Salzburg.

Hallein

Keltenmuseum
Pflegerplatz 5; tel: 06245-807 83; www.keltenmuseum.at; daily 9am–5pm; entrance charge; map p.135 C2
The excellent and newly displayed Celtic Museum exhibits the valuable archaeological finds, including tools and equipment used by the early miners, as well as priceless burial gifts. The museum is housed in the former administrative building (1654), now given a modern facelift, of the mining and salt works commission of the prince-archbishops; other sections are devoted to the history of the town and local customs and guilds.

The Salzkammergut

Bauernmuseum
Hilfbergstrasse 5, Mondsee; tel: 0664-340 6020; www.museummondsee.at; Tue–Sun, May–Aug: 10am–6pm, Sept: 10am–5pm, Oct: Sat–Sun

10am–5pm; entrance charge; map p.135 E4

At Mondsee, a number of traditional farm buildings are run in accordance with historical research, giving visitors a window onto 18th-century Austrian life. A particular attraction at the open-air Freilichtmuseum is the Rauchhaus, a working 'smokehouse' responsible for curing meat from the farm's livestock, which can be sampled in the museum shop.

Fahrzeugmuseum
Sulzbach 178, Bad Ischl; tel: 06132-26658; www.fahrzeugmuseum.at; daily Apr–Oct: 9am–6pm; entrance charge; map p.137 D2

For those who prefer to speed out of Austro-nostalgia into the age of high technology, a world of chrome and steel is offered by the Fahrzeugmuseum (vehicle museum) a short way out of Bad Ischl. Here are gathered planes, motorcycles, steam locomotives and military vehicles from World War II and beyond.

Kammerhofmuseum
Kammerhofgasse 8, Gmunden; tel: 07612-794 420; Wed–Sun 10am–5pm; www.gmunden. ooe.gv.at; entrance charge; map p.137 E2

Gmunden's Kammerhofmuseum is a regional museum, with an emphasis on the regional rather than the national, and, appropriately for an institution located within a former salt exchange, devoted to the trade which made the region great. There are a number of models on display and the region's famous ceramic makes more than an appearance. The museum has recently been completely overhauled and the exhibits are beautifully displayed. The museum also includes the more eccentric **Klo & So Sanitärmuseum**. This tribute to the German-speaking world's fascination with human excreta moves from the limited facilities offered by Alpine hunters' huts through discreet bourgeois constructions of the 19th century to ornate imperial bidets and basins and enema apparatuses of eye-watering design.

Also in Bad Ischl, the Photomuseum in the Kaiservilla gardens houses a series of exhibits on the history of the camera, in addition to a collection of *fin-de-siècle* photographs. It is housed in a marble folly built as a garden retreat for Franz Josef's Empress. www.kaiservilla.at. *(See Castles and Palaces, p.47.)*

KZ-Gedenkstätte und Zeitgeschichte Museum Ebensee
Kirchengasse 5, Ebensee; tel: 06133-5601; www.memorial-ebensee.at; Jan–Oct, Tue–Sun 10am–5pm, Nov–Dec Tue–Fri 10am–5pm; entrance charge includes entry to the nearby concentration camp memorial; map p.137 E2

Ebensee's museum of Zeitgeschichte, or contemporary history, like many across provincial Austria, tells the story of the modern state from the fall of the Habsburg Empire to the present day. For a country like Austria, whose post-imperial existence has been a confused journey from rump state to core EU member via periods of Cold War neutrality and Nazi annexation, such museums are vital markers of national identity. What distinguishes the Ebensee institution is its clear-eyed and critical approach to the darker aspects of the Austrian story, including later generations' claim that Austria was a victim of German Nazism.

Musikinstrumente-Museum der Völker
Aberseestrasse 11, St Gilgen;

Right: Celtic displays at the Hallstatt Museum.

Left: exhibits at Hallein's Keltenmuseum, *see p.101*.

tel: 0622-78235; www.salzburg.gv.at; June–Oct: Tue–Sun 9–11am, 3–7pm, Oct–Jan: Mon–Fri 9–11am, 2–5pm, Jan–May Mon–Thur 9–11am, 3–6pm, Fri 9–11am, Sun 3–6pm; map p.135 E3

The folk instrument museum, which brings together instruments from around the world, was originally the private collection of the Zur Eck family (and still under the curatorship of family member Askold), it was donated to the local community in 1997 and currently comprises some 1,800 instruments, from the valuable to the exotic and downright bizarre. Staff are always eager to play the instruments and visitors may be lucky enough to receive an impromptu demonstration.

Museum Zinkenbacher
Aberseestrasse 11, St Gilgen; tel: 0676-743 0916; daily July–Sept: 3–7pm; map p.135 E3

In the same building as the Museum der Völker *(above)*, the Museum Zinkenbacher celebrates the history of the artists' colony which was established in St Gilgen in the 1920s and 30s. Although the circle which formed the colony disbanded in 1938, the museum, founded in 2001

At Schloss Scharnstein, outside Gmunden, a 16th-century construction houses a number of museums, covering Austrian history, crime and policing, as well as an extensive collection of reptiles and insects *(see Castles and Palaces, p.48)*.

after six years' agitation by a society of supporters, devotes itself to preserving the legacy of the colony beyond its mere physical products, having located in 2002 the last surviving artist, Lisel Salzer, who had been forced to emigrate to the United States in 1939.

Stadtmuseum Bad Ischl
Esplanade 10, Bad Ischl; tel: 06132-25476; www.stadtmuseum.at; Jan–Mar: Fri–Sun 10am–5pm, Apr–Jun, Sept–Oct, Dec: Wed 2–7pm, Fri 1–5pm, Sat–Sun 10am–5pm, Jul–Aug: Wed 2–7pm, Fri 1–5pm, Thur, Sat–Sun 10am–5pm; entrance charge; map p.137 D2

Bad Ischl's Stadtmuseum, on the esplanade in Franz Josef's resort town of choice, was once the site of a hotel which entertained the Habsburg princes. Today the museum seems to symbolise modern Austria's integration of past and present as it houses a working registry office as well as exhibits on

the town, a collection of curios from the Far East and displays of regional dress which chronicle the adoption of clothes associated with the peasantry as part of Austria's national formalwear. Also part of the museum is the **Lehár-Villa**, home of the famous operetta composer (May–Jun, Sept: Wed–Sun 10am–5pm, Jul–Aug also Mon).

Hallstatt

Stadtmuseum
Seestrasse 56, Hallstatt; tel: 06134-8280 15; www.museum-hallstatt.at; daily May–Sept: 10am–6pm, Oct: 10am–4pm, Nov–Mar: Wed–Sun 11am–3pm; entrance charge; map p.137 D1

Hallstatt's Stadtmuseum is attractive and highly up-to-date, with motion-sensitive multimedia display and thoughtful reconstructions that include a traditional kitchen, mineshaft, a giant Beinhaus skull, an archaeological dig and even a room-shaking simulated avalanche which all children, bar the very youngest, will love. The exhibit devoted to prehistoric excrement, complete with sample under magnification, may be no surprise to those familiar with the Germanic fascination with human waste, but offers a surprisingly profound analysis of early Hallstatt diet and lifestyle.

Music

If Austria has a claim to artistic fame it is surely in the field of music. The list of musicians and composers from the Western classical canon who were born, or who have lived and worked, in Austria is quite staggering. They include: Mozart, Haydn, Beethoven, Schubert, Brahms, Bruckner, Mahler, Schoenberg, Berg and Webern. Austrian music is not, however, limited to the works we hear in the concert hall or opera house, there are also strong traditions of liturgical, folk and popular music, many of which fed into and had a significant impact on the works of the composers mentioned above.

Gluck and Mozart

Until the empress Maria Theresa discovered Christoph Willibald von Gluck (1714–87), whose reformist works (starting with *Alkestis*, 1767) subordinated the music to dramatic requirements, music in Austria was dominated to a large extent by Italian composers.

Gluck was succeeded by Salzburg's most famous son, Wolfgang Amadeus Mozart (1756–91), regarded as one of the greatest of all western composers for his sense of melody, form and his success across all contemporary genres, from piano sonatas, to symphonies and opera.

His musical talents had been recognised at a very early age, he was composing by the age of five, and he and his sister Nannerl were taken around the courts of Europe performing keyboard duets. After travels around Italy he joined the employ of the prince-archbishop of Salzburg, but this did not suit his temperament and, after literally being booted out by the chamberlain, he settled in

Above: the composer Michael Haydn.

Vienna in 1781 where he largely remained until his early death.

After his move to Vienna, much of his musical activity was in aristocratic salons, where his piano and chamber works were performed. However, his greatest public successes, apart from occasional concerts, were in the opera house. His most popular opera in his homeland was *Die Zauberflöte*, but he was, however, occasionally less successful at court, the emperor complaining ironically that *Die Entführung aus dem Serail* was 'too beautiful

for our ears… and with very many notes'. When he was appointed to the court his salary was 800 Gulden a year, as compared to the 2,000 Gluck had received. 'It is,' said Mozart, 'too much for what I do, and not enough for what I can do.'

Joseph and Michael Haydn

Mozart's mentor was Joseph Haydn (1732–1809), a former chorister at St Stephen's, who worked for the Esterházy princes as Kapellmeister and was treated more or less like a servant. It was this position within the household that accounts for his extraordinary output. This comprises some 113 symphonies, 47 keyboard sonatas, 68 string quartets and some 23 stage works (mostly operas). His music, still one of the staples of the concert hall, is infused with a great deal of wit, but also a deep humanity. His operas, largely written for his patron, were popular in his day but have been rarely performed since his death (although the music is of undoubted genius

Left: Riccardo Muti conducts the Wiener Philharmoniker at the Mozart celebrations in Salzburg in 2006.

ditions of Mozart and Haydn (the so-called *Wiener Klassik*), he not only developed these but also pushed at the boundaries of form, harmony and melody, looking forward to the ideals of Romanticism. His individuality was, in part, a product of his own unhappy life and deafness, an affliction which increasingly cut him off from the world, a process which, while discernible in his works, did not lessen his concern for the human condition.

His legacy remains in, among other works, his nine symphonies, 32 piano sonatas, five piano concertos, and the opera *Fidelio*. From the revolutionary fervour of the third ('Eroica') symphony, to the programmatic nature of the sixth (with birdcalls and a peasant's dance), to the grand statement of the ninth and Schiller's *Ode to Joy*, Beethoven sets the scene for many of the concerns of the Romantic movement, and hence his importance for many later composers of the 19th century.

Beethoven was hero-worshipped by his near contemporary Franz Schubert (1797–1828), who might be seen as the first fully-fledged Romantic composer. In his wonderful chamber music and *Lieder*, gentle lyricism alternates with deep and sometimes melancholy passion, and whose *Schubertiades* (musical soirées at which he played his latest compositions to friends) are seen as typical of the burgher idyll of the Biedermeier period (1814–48).

He spent the rest of his life in the city and was organist and Kapellmeister at the court of the archbishop.
SEE ALSO MUSEUMS AND GALLERIES, P.99

Beethoven

The third of the trio of the great Austrian classical composers along with Mozart and Joseph Haydn, is Ludwig van Beethoven (1770–1827). This towering figure was born in Bonn, Germany, but moved to Vienna in 1792 where he spent the rest of his life. The inheritor of the Viennese tra-

the plots often leave something to be desired).

Towards the end of his life he managed to free himself a little from the constraints of his employer and not only started to get his music played further afield but also undertook a trip to London, which not only brought him wider European acclaim, but made him a lot of money.

His brother, the lesser-known composer Michael (1737–1806) was to settle in Salzburg in 1763, where there is a museum to his memory.

Below: Mozart's piano in the museum dedicated to his life in Salzburg.

Brahms and Bruckner

The 19th century saw the Austrian musical world divide between followers of the 'pure' tradition of Beethoven and the 'modernists' who were followers of composers such as Liszt and Wagner. The two standard bearers of this struggle were Johannes Brahms, the last representative of Romantic Viennese classicism in the tradition of Beethoven, and Anton Bruckner, a mild-mannered, even saintly individual, who was taken up by the supporters of Wagner. The battle was carried on more by hangers-on than the composers themselves (although Brahms did once describe the music of Bruckner as 'symphonic boa-constrictors, the amateurish, confused and illogical abortions of a rustic schoolmaster'), who on the one hand accused Brahms of being reactionary, and on the other accused Bruckner of being long-winded and incompetent. The greatest malice came from the immensely influential critic Eduard Hanslick (memorably pilloried by Wagner as the pretentious and talentless Beckmesser in *Die Meistersinger von Nürnberg*) who was entirely on Brahms's side.

Both great symphonists, Brahms writes works that are the summation of a tradition, with a consummate mastery of the form and harmony of the Viennese classics, allied with his melodic technique of continuous variation, and produced some of the most finely and logically wrought pieces of the 19th century, but also ones that are intensely moving. Like the other great Austrian classicists, he dominated several

forms: he was a symphonist, wrote *Lieder*, chamber music and produced a huge amount of piano music. In contrast, Bruckner was brought up as a choirboy at the monastery of St Florian and was later the abbey organist. The symphonies cover huge sweeps of time and, with Bruckner's acute sense of drama and form, often build to shattering climaxes, yet he was also capable of creating the most exquisitely delicate passages.

Mahler and Strauss

One of Bruckner's pupils at the Conservatory (although they were ill-suited) was Gustav Mahler (1860–1911), now seen as one of the greatest late-19th century symphonic composers. However, his works were not widely appreciated in Austria during his lifetime and, as a Jewish composer, his achievements were also obscured by the rise of the Nazis in Austria and Germany. Furthermore, he had also made enemies – many of them fuelled by anti-Semitism – during his tenure of the directorship of the Vienna Hofoper (1898–1907).

Ironically, perhaps one of the most 'Austrian' works of the time was Richard Strauss's opera *Der Rosenkavalier* (1913), written by a German living in Garmisch whose first performance was given in Dresden. However, its use of the Viennese waltz throughout not only provides a unifying motif but imparts a uniquely Austrian flavour to the whole piece. This use of the waltz was a stroke of genius on Strauss's part, and it merges beautifully with Hugo von Hofmannsthal's delightfully witty libretto. Fittingly, given Hofmannsthal's involvement in setting up the festival, it was

Left: it is hard to escape from Mozart in the city of his birth.

with *Der Rosenkavalier* that the new Grosser Festspiel-haus was opened at the 1960 Salzburg Festival.
SEE ALSO FESTIVALS, P.69

Modernism

After the death of Mahler a revolutionary new direction was set by the theorist and composer Arnold Schoen-berg (1874–1951). His experiments lead him to abandon tonality altogether in an 'emancipation of disso-nance'. His first atonal works are Expressionist (Schoen-berg was also a painter), though he later codified his ideas into the more classicist style of serial composition.

His serial ideas (in which all 12 notes of the chromatic scale are given equal promi-nence) were most fully devel-oped by his two distinguished students, Anton von Webern (1883–1945) and Alban Berg (1885–1935). Webern was ruthlessly logical, creating exquisite and sparse mina-tures, whereas Berg was far more atuned to Expression-ism, seen to best advantage in his two operas *Wozzeck* (1922) and *Lulu* (unfinished), or a serial neo-Romanticism, as heard in his late violin con-certo (1935).

Folk and Popular Musics

By the 19th century system-atic collection of *Volkslied* (folksong) had started. This was, in part, a response to a greater awareness of sup-posed national identities, and by the end of the century had become an important com-ponent of the nascent nation-alisms that were sweeping the Austro-Hungarian Empire.

They were responsible for introducing a mediated ver-sion of *Volkslied* into the urban domestic sphere and the con-cert hall. Arranged versions of the songs were given piano accompaniment, and made into choral arrangements. One result of this was a concentra-tion on certain genres, such as the Alpine Jodler (yodelling) which were performed in pop-ular concerts by singers wear-ing traditional dress.

A highly mediated form of Austrian folk music emerged in the 1970s, known dis-paragingly as *Lederhosen-musik*, and was broadcast widely on television both at home and abroad. This bland, kitschy conflagration of, largely, Alpine syles was per-formed by groups of tradition-ally clad instrumentalists (on clarinet, trumpet, tuba, accor-dian, guitar and drums) and

sometimes a singer. It did much to promote a chocolate box and *Sound of Music* image of the country, but little to preserve and accord respect for the country's traditions.

A reaction against this came with the pan-regional genre, Alpine punk. Initially starting in Bavaria in the 1970s, and then spreading to Austria, it took elements of traditonal Alpine musics and gave them a twist by adding satirical lyrics, electronics (as both amplification and distor-tion) and driving rhythms. This injected dynamism back into the traditional music scene and it has slowly started to revive. A good source of these types of music is the archive of the Österreichisches Volkliedw-erk (www.volks liedwerk.at).

Music Shops

Mayrische Musikalien-handlung

Theatergasse, A-5020; tel: 0662-873 596; www.mayrische.at; Mon–Fri 9am– 6pm, Sat 9am–3pm; map p.132 C3
Salzburg had to have a great music shop, and this is it. A huge selection of books and scores, which they will also send out by post.

Music Venues

SEE FESTIVALS, P.70–1

Below: the region has a strong tradition of brass band playing.

Restaurants

Although, on the whole, Salzburg is a relatively expensive city, eating in a restaurant remains quite cheap. There are, of course, the top-notch establishments where the generally excellent food is expensive, but on the whole you will be able to eat delicious meals at reasonable prices. Summer, if the weather allows, is the time for eating outdoors. Many restaurants have gardens in the summer or, at the very least, tables on the pavement. Remember, however, that the city is in the foothills of the Alps and that even in summer there are very few evenings when you will not need a sweater or jacket.

The Mönchsberg

Augustiner Bräustübl
Lindhofstrasse 7; tel: 0662-431 246; www.augustinerbier.at; €; Mon–Fri 3–11pm, Sat–Sun 2.30–11pm; bus: 7, 20, 21, 24, 27, 28; map p.132 A4
Genuine beer-hall atmosphere in a brewery founded by Augustinian monks. Wonderful beer, beautiful garden and plenty of snacks from the stands; lots of traditional sausage, roast pork and radishes. You can even bring your own picnic.

Magazin
Augustinergasse 13; tel: 0662-841 5840; www.magazin.co.at; €€–€€€; Mon–Sat noon–10pm; bus: 7, 20, 21, 24, 27, 28; map p.132 A3
This trendy new eatery with a deli and cook shop attached serves up tasty, if pricey, international dishes with an Austrian twist.
SEE ALSO FOOD AND DRINK, P.76

Prices for an average three-course meal with wine:
€€€ over €50
€€ €25–€50
€ under €25

Above: chic interior at the Museum der Moderne's M32.

M32
Museum der Moderne, Mönchsberg 32; tel: 0662-841 000; http://m32.at; €€; Tue–Sat 9am–1am, open Mon during Festival; map p.132 B3
The Museum of Modern Art has this chic restaurant with what must be the best view in the city. The modern European dishes include a lot of pasta and fish, well cooked and tasty, and there is a good wine list. Excellent for breakfast and also just to drop in for coffee.

The Altstadt

Bärenwirt
Müllnerhauptstrasse 8; tel: 0662-422 404; www.baerenwirt-salzburg.at; €€; daily 11am–11pm; bus: 7, 20, 21, 24, 27, 28; map p.132 B4
As well as providing Augustiner beer on tap, this is a traditional restaurant serving Austrian cuisine, vegetarian and wholegrain food. There has been an eatery on this site for over 350 years.

Blaue Gans
Getreidegasse 41–3, tel: 0662-8424 910; www.blauegans.at; €€€; Mon–Sat noon–10pm; map p.132 B3
The restaurant of this central design hotel produces some excellent classic Austrian dishes such as stewed cheek of pork and fried char. In season there is often local game as well. The outdoor seating on Herbert-von-Karajan-Platz is very popular during the summer. However, if that is full you can get often get a seat inside.

Carpe Diem
Getreidegasse 50; tel: 0662-848 800; www.carpediemfinest fingerfood.com; €€€; Mon–Sat

Left: the excellent restaurant of the Goldener Hirsch.

floor overlooking Alter Markt; in the summer they have tables down in the square.

Esszimmer
Müllnerhauptstrasse 33, tel: 870 899; www.esszimmer.com; €€€; Tue–Sat noon–2pm, 6.30–9.30pm, also Mon during the Festival; bus: 7, 20, 21, 24, 27, 28; map p.132 A4

Fine dining in a lovely location. This restaurant has an excellent reputation, and has picked up a number of awards on the way, and its relaxed atmosphere makes it a popular place. Vegetarians are well catered for and there is a quiet garden in summer.

Herzl
Hotel Goldener Hirsch, Getreidegasse 37; tel: 0662-808 4824; www.goldenerhirsch.com; €€€; daily 10.30am–10pm; map p.132 B3

This famous restaurant in the hotel of the same name specialises in Austrian cuisine. Over the years it has won numerous accolades for its food and is the place to go for a special occasion. The *Tafelspitz* and *Nockerl* are works of art and there are always daily specials, such as local wild mushrooms.

8.30am–midnight; map p.132 B3

This is the first floor restaurant above the 'Fingerfood' café on Salzburg's main shopping street. It claims to specialise in traditional dishes, some of them updated, but there is a distinctly Italian feel to the menu. That said, the food is good and the surroundings very pleasant.

Coco Lezzone
Franz Josef Kai 7; tel: 0662-846 735; www.cocolezzone.at; €€; Mon–Fri 11am–2pm,

5.30–11pm, Sat–Sun 5.30–11pm; bus: 7, 20, 21, 24, 27, 28; map p.132 B3

Although this Italian stalwart churns out all the usual pasta and main courses, the pizzas are the best thing on offer here. Avoid the rather bland 'Indian' dishes.

Da Pippo
Alter Markt 2, tel: 0662-843 861; www.pippo.deu.at; €€; daily 11.30am–11pm; map p.132 C3

Good Italian food with a buffet of cold starters and occasional live piano music while you eat. Located on the first

Below: a Humboldt ice-cream menu…

Below: and daily specials.

Above: eating out at the Wildermann.

Above: more than one use for a beer glass at Krimpelstätter.

Hotel Restaurant Elefant

Sigmund-Haffner-Gasse 4; tel: 0662-8433 97; www.elefant.at; €€; Mon–Sat 11am–11pm, open Sun during Festival; map p.132 C3

A pleasant restaurant with nice wooden tables and decorations. The Austrian dishes, such as *Backhändel* (roast chicken) and *Schnitzel* are well turned out. A good place for families to eat.

Humboldt Stubn'

Gstättengasse 4–6; tel: 0662-843 197; www.humboldt stubn.at; €–€€; daily 10am–1am; map p.132 B3

Despite being cloaked in the garb of Austrian traditionalism, this is in fact one of the most modern and exciting venues in the city today. With good music and an energetic bar staff, it is a great place for a fun night out, or for independent travellers to hook up with like-minded hedonists.

Il Sole

Gstättengasse 15; tel: 0662-843 284; €–€€; daily summer and winter 11.30am–3pm, 5.30–midnight, closed Tue autumn and spring; map p.132 B3

The Italian cooking on offer here is tasty and uncomplicated, offering excellent value for money and a useful, reliably good refuelling stop near the Mönchsberg lift. Look out for the daily specials.

Indigo

Rudolfskai 8; tel: 0662-843 480; www.indigofood.com; €; Mon–Sat 10am–10pm, Sun noon–9pm; bus: 7, 20, 21, 24, 27, 28; map p.132 C3

The most central of a chain of small fast-food establishments that are excellent if you want a quick snack during the day while sightseeing. They offer Thai and vegetarian cuisine and some locations have indoor seating. Most restaurants are non-smoking.

K+K Restaurant am Waagplatz

Waagplatz 2; tel: 0662-842 156; www.kkhotels.com; €€–€€€; daily 10am–10.30pm, til midnight during the Festival; map p.132 C3

This large restaurant, with different specialities on each floor, is popular with tourists and can get a bit noisy when tour groups descend. Nevertheless, the food is decent and the atmosphere friendly

enough. Dishes ranges from Austrian classics to South and East Asian food.

Krimpelstätter

Müllnerhauptstrasse 31; tel: 0662-432 274; www.krimpelstaetter.at; €€; Mon–Sat 11am–midnight; bus: 7, 20, 21, 24, 27, 28; map p.132 A4

A traditional tavern with a beer garden serving good Austrian food. Very popular with the festival crowd.

Maredo

Judengasse 5–7; tel: 0662-843 894; www.maredo.at; €€; daily 11.30am–11.30pm; map p.132 C3

Fast and friendly service in this brightly lit steak and seafood restaurant. The steak and prawns can be recommended. Useful if you want to eat early.

Nagano

Griesgasse 19; tel: 0662-849 488; €€; daily 11.30am–3pm, 5.30–11pm; map p.132 B3

A sushi restaurant situated in the centre of the Old Town. There is a wide choice, including meat dishes, all served in wooden boxes. The lunch deals are particularly good.

Nordsee

Getreidegasse 11; tel: 0662-844 978; www.nordsee.com; €–€€; daily 10am–7pm; map p.132 B3

Part of a chain of country-wide seafood restaurants. Good, quick meals for those who need to maximise sightseeing time.

Pan e Vin

Gstättengasse 1; tel: 0662-8446 6614; www.panevin.at; €€–€€€; daily 11am–11pm; map p.132 B3

The menu at this high-end contemporary restaurant combines ingredients and styles across nations to offer a broadly imagined Mediterranean cuisine, excellently prepared from the freshest ingredients. The modern, but

warm décor serves to com-
plement both the cooking
style and the traditions of
the 600-year-old building
which houses it. Well worth
treating yourself.

Republic
Anton-Neumayr-Platz 2;
tel: 0662-841 613;
www.republic.at; €–€€; daily
8am–1am, kitchen closes
11pm; map p.132 B3
Not only is the restaurant
menu innovative and exciting
at this good-value venue, but
the bar food is also excellent,
helping you sustain yourself
through an evening's drinking
and carousing if you so desire.

Paul-Stube
Herrengasse 16; tel: 0662-843
220; www.paul-stube.at; €–€€;
Mon–Thur 5pm–1am, Fri–Sat
5pm–2am; map p.133 C2
Situated in one of the narrow little alleys below the
fortress, this is an old,
traditional restaurant serving
Austrian food and good
salads. There is a very
pleasant garden in the
summer, too.

Stiftskeller St Peter
St Peter Bezkirk 1/4; tel: 0662-
841 2680; www.haslauer.at;
€€–€€€; daily 10.30am–
midnight, kitchen closes
10.45pm, later during the Festival; map p.132 B2
Founded as long ago as 803
this historic restaurant is one
of the oldest in Austria. The
cosy interior is good for a
romantic meal and the Austrian dishes, especially the
Tafelspitz and *Salzburger
Nockerl*, are very good. You
can also eat in an ornate
Baroque hall while a selection
of Mozart's greatest hits is

performed by musicians in
fancy dress.

Triangel
Wiener-Philharmoniker-Gasse 7;
tel: 0662-842 229;
www.triangel-salzburg.at;
€–€€; daily 11am–midnight;
map p.132 C3
A tavern-style restaurant
popular with students and
concert goers, close to the
Festival Halls. It has a cosy
interior, and outdoor seating
in summer. Traditional Austrian dishes include *Beuschel*
and *Schnitzel*, and there is
also pasta and good
desserts.

Wildermann
Getreidegasse 20; tel: 0662-841
787; www.wildermann.co.at; €;
Mon–Sat 10am–11pm, kitchen
closes 9pm, later during the

Festival; map p.132 B3
This historic Gasthaus has
long wooden tables to share
with the locals. The menu is
Austrian and the portions are
huge. Among a range of
good dishes the *Schnitzel* is
recommended.

Zipfer Bierhaus
Universitätsplatz 19; tel: 0662-
840 745; www.zipfer-bier
haus.at; €–€€; Mon–Sat 10am–
midnight; map p.132 B3
In a 15th-century building,
this traditional tavern serves
Austrian food and beer in
beer-hall style. The décor is
quaintly old-fashioned and
there is an old well to have a
look at in the basement.

Zirkelwirt
Pfeifergasse 14; tel: 0662–843
472; www.zirkel-wirt.at; €;

Below: the entrance to Stiftskeller St Peter.

Above: the ever-popular Triangel, *see p.111*

Mon–Thur 4pm–1am, Fri–Sat 5pm–1am; map p.133 C3
This Austrian tavern has an international twist and fabulous meals at affordable prices. Or you can just go for a coffee or a beer.

The New Town

Ährlich
Wolf-Dietrich-Strasse 7; tel: 0662-8712 7560; www.biohotel.cc; €€; Tue–Sat 6–11pm; bus: 2, 4, 21, 22; map p.133 C4
Set in a hotel, this claims to being Salzburg's first eaterie to consciously offer vegetarian food, this organic restaurant offers a range of options for vegetarians and their meat-eating fellows alike.

Andreas Hofer Weinstube
Steingasse 65; tel: 0662-872 769; www.dieweinstube.at; €–€€; Mon–Sat 6pm–1am, also Sun in Dec; bus: 20, 25, 28, 840; map p.133 D3
This wine bar not only has a good range of Austrian wines but also dishes up decent local food.

Bali Restaurant
Paris-Lodron-Strasse 22; tel: 0662-872 297; www.restaurant-bali.at; Tue–Sun 11.30am–2.30pm, 6pm–2am; €€; bus: 2, 4, 21, 22; map p.133 C4
This restaurant serves excellent Indonesian food which stands out among the rival regional eateries. A seriously chilled-out ambiance (heavy on the bamboo), plus easy-going staff offering atypically informal Austrian *Gastfreundlichkeit* (hospitality), complement the Austrian

beers on tap, and the Balinese variants which are served by the bottle.

Bangkok
Bayerhamerstrasse 33; tel: 0662-873 688; www.restaurant-bangkok.at; €–€€; Tue–Sun 11.30am–2.30pm, 5.30–11.30pm; bus: 22; map p.134 C3
The menu of Thai cuisine on offer at the quiet, comfy Bangkok is pretty authentic by comparison to the many Asian restaurants which adjust to conservative Austrian palates.

Daimler's
Giselakai 17; tel: 0662-873 967; http://www.mein daimlers.at; €€; Tue–Wed 7.30pm–2am, Thur–Sat 7.30pm–4am; bus: 3, 5, 6, 7, 8, 20, 25, 28, 840; map p.132 C3
This grill is located in the same building as a bustling local bar, it offers a beautiful view of the River Salzach to accompany your food; which is American-oriented, filling and tasty.

Die Weisse
Rupertgasse 10; tel: 0662-872 246; www.dieweisse.at; €€; Mon–Sat 10.30am–midnight; bus: 4; map p.133 D4
An attractive restaurant with themed décor in each of its dining rooms, Die Weisse has more to offer than pretty interior design; it also houses a microbrewery whose trademark *Weissbier* (cloudy wheat beer with the yeast not brewed out) makes a perfect accompaniment to the Austrian staples on offer here.

Gablerbräu
Linzergasse 9; tel: 0662-889 65; www.gablerbrau.com; €; daily 11.30am–11pm; bus: 4; map p.132 C3
This restaurant is located on the ground floor of the eponymous hotel on Linzergasse. A welcoming bar, decorated with photo portraits of

Prices for an average three-course meal with wine:
€€€ over €50
€€ €25–€50
€ under €25

jazz legends, provides a convenient spot to sip on a beer before passing through to a tavern-style restaurant which also includes salad and antipasti buffets.

Mirabell
Auerspergstrasse 4;
tel: 0662-8899 94005;
www.starwoodhotels.com; €€;
daily 6.30–10am, noon–2pm,
6.30– 9.30pm; bus: 22; map
p.132 B4
This restaurant, within the Sheraton hotel, offers food of a high standard, including all the traditional Austrian staples but also a witty bistro menu including Alpine tapas and a tongue-in-cheek 'Salzburger burger'.

Shakespeare
Hubert-Sattler-Gasse 3; tel: 0662-879 106; www.shakespeare.at;
€; daily 9am–2am, kitchen closes 10.30, later during the Festival;
bus: 21, 22; map p.132 C4
Unashamedly aiming for a clientele of students and aspiring bohemians, the emphasis at the Shakespeare is less on a ground-breaking menu – although the international cuisine on offer is perfectly competent – than a friendly, studenty atmosphere, aided by the late opening hours and cheap beer.

Spicy Spices
Wolf Dietrich Strasse 1; tel:
0662-870 712; €; Mon–Fri
11.30am–9.30pm, Sat–Sun
noon–9.30pm; bus: 2, 4, 21, 22;
map p.133 C4
One more vegetarian option for visitors to Salzburg's New Town. A wide range of tastily prepared health foods on offer, particularly Indian

dishes. Take-aways and an express lunch menu are also available.

Taj Mahal
Bayerhamerstrasse 13;
tel: 0662-882 010;
www.restaurant-tajmahal.com;
€€; Tue–Fri, Sun 11.30am–2pm, 5.30–11pm, Sat
5.30–11pm; bus: 22;
map p.133 C4
This Indian restaurant is a comfortable place to pass the evening in the jovial company of students and travellers. Visitors should be warned that Austro-Indian cooking, like the Austro-Chinese, is somewhat toned down for the Salzburgers' taste buds.

Wasserfall
Linzergasse 10; tel: 0662-873 331; www.restaurant-wasserfall.at; €€; daily 5pm–midnight; bus: 4; map p.132 C3
The food is good at this Italian restaurant, but the principal attraction is the subterranean setting, complete with the stream which gives the 'Waterfall' its name passing between the tables.

Zum Fidelen Affen
Priesterhausgasse 8; tel: 0662-877 361; Mon–Sat 5pm–11pm,

later during the Festival; €–€€;
bus: 4; map p.132 C3
Widely acknowledged among both travellers and locals as an outstanding spot for traditional food, the reputation of this restaurant is aided by the deliberately tavern-styled décor and the numerous, good-humoured regulars.

Around Salzburg
ARGEBeisel
Josef-Preis-Allee 16; tel: 0662-840 839; www.argebeisl.at; €€;
Mon–Fri 11.30am–10pm, Sat
5–10pm, bar and café open
later; bus: 5, 25; map p.133 D2
This restaurant is in Salzburg's newish cultural centre. The food concentrates on modern versions of classical Austrian dishes.

Friesacher
Hellbrunnerstrasse 17; Anif; tel:
06246-89770; www.hotel
friesacher.com; €€; daily
11.30am–10.30pm; bus: 25;
map p.133 D2
Freisacher has an excellent reputation as one of the best traditional restaurants serving Austrian food, wine and beer. Although slightly out of the city in Anif, it is worth making the journey here, particularly if you are visiting Hellbrunn.

Below: beer, beer, more beer…

Below: the *Zirkelwirt*, *see p.111.*

Ikarus
Hangar-7, Wilhelm-Spazier-Strasse 7a; tel: 0662-219 777; www.hangar-7.com; €€€; daily noon–2pm, 7–10pm; bus: 2; map p.134 C3

This is a restaurant with a difference. Enjoy a first-class meal with a view of the Red Bull collection of vintage aircraft in Hangar-7. Top guest chefs from around the world spend a month at a time cooking up delights. Reservations are necessary.

Lemon Chilli
Nonntaler Hauptstrasse 24; tel: 0662-842 558; www.lemon chilli.at; €€; Mon–Fri 11am–late, Sat–Sun from 4pm; bus: 5; map p.133 C2

A Tex-Mex restaurant where the kitchen turns out good food and the bar creates excellent cocktails; all amid a lively atmosphere. Popular with students, and there is garden in the summer. Reservations recommended.

Lin's Garden
Leopoldskronstrasse 1, tel: 846 356; www.linsgarden.at; €€; Tue–Sun 11.30am–2.30pm, 5.30–midnight; bus: 21, 22; map p.132 A2

Very friendly Chinese restaurant a few minutes' walk from the Old Town. It has a charming walled garden and excellent dim-sum lunch offers.

Poseidon
Neutorstrasse 34; tel: 0662-842 918; www.restaurant-poseidon.co.at; €€; daily 11.30am–3pm, 5.30pm–1am; bus: 1, 4, 22; map p.132 A3

Probably Salzburg's best Greek restaurant. It is very popular and reservations are recommended. All your favourite Greek dishes served in warm and welcoming surroundings. There is a lovely garden in the summer.

Restaurant Riedenburg
Neutorstrasse 31, tel: 0662-830 815; www.riedenburg.at; €€€; Tue–Sat noon–2pm, 6pm–midnight, open daily during the Festival; bus: 1, 4, 22; map p.132 A2

This is considered by some to be the best restaurant in Salzburg. It serves wonderful Austrian food, beautifully presented. The wine and Schnapps list are also exquisite. Reservations recommended.

Schloss Aigen
Schwarzenbergpromenade 37, Aigen; tel: 0662-621 284; www.schloss-aigen.at; €€–€€€; Thur 6–10pm, Fri–Sat, Mon noon–2pm, 6–10pm, Sun noon–10pm; map p.135 C3

This elegant restaurant speicalises in local organic beef, served in a *Suppentopf* (broth with vegetables) with the classic side helpings of *Apfelkren* and a chive sauce. There are also some good modern Austrian dishes and a lovely garden to eat them in.

Wastlwirt
Rochusgasse 15; tel: 0662-820 100; www.wastlwirt.com; €€; Mon–Fri noon–2pm, 6–10pm; bus: 27; map p.134 C3

Located in a quiet corner, not far from the city centre, this traditional tavern – serving the usual selection of Austrian dishes – is wonderfully cosy with lots of wood and a leafy, shady garden.

Prices for an average three-course meal with wine:
€€€ over €50
€€ €25–€50
€ under €25

Left: Die Weisse, *see p.112.*

Above: Zipfer, *see p.111.*

Above: the excellent Friesacher, *see p.113.*

Salzkammergut

BAD ISCHL
Franz Lehár Restaurant
Kongresshaus, Kurpark; tel: 06132-233 22; www.kongress haus.badischl.at; €€€; May–Oct daily 10am–10pm; map p.137 D2
Travel back in time to the heyday of the imperial spa resort by entering the beautifully laid gardens of the Kurpark and dining at this villa at its centre. Here atmosphere is everything, although the food is not bad either, with classical quartets playing in the pavilion and a true *königlich und kaiserlich* (imperial and royal) service from the staff.

GMUNDEN
Orth Stub'n
Seeschloss Orth, Orth 1; tel: 07612-624 99; www.schloss orth.com; €€€; May–Sept: Mon–Sat 11.30am–2pm, 6–10pm, Sun 11.30am–2pm, Oct–Apr: Tue–Sat 11.30am–2pm, 6–10pm, Sun 11.30am–2pm; map p.137 E3
This soap-opera-starring castle now is the location of an award-winning restaurant. The menu focuses on modern Austrian dishes with the odd nod towards Italy. Of course, the surroundings are lovely.

ST GILGEN
Fischer-Wirt
Ischlerstrase 21; tel: 06227-2304; www.fischer-wirt.at; €€–€€€; Apr–Jun, Sept–Oct: Tue–Sun, also Mon Jul–Aug; map p.135 E3
Even in a region of lakes where every restaurant that can claim a sight-line to the water's edge prides itself on the freshness of its fish, this is an outstanding restaurant which works wonders with the excellent-quality local catch. As well as single plate options, a shared platter allows diners to sample the full selection of fishy fare.

ST WOLFGANG
Im Weissen Rössl
Im Weissen Rössl, Im Stöckl 74; tel: 06138-230 60; www.weissesroessl.at; €€€; daily, summer: 9am–10pm, winter: 10am–6.30pm; map p.137 D2
This hotel tavern was the setting for *The White Horse Inn*, an operetta dear to the Austrian heart. The name alone guarantees a steady stream of custom for the owners, although this has not made them complacent and both the terrace and tavern here offer food of a good standard.

The Salzach and High Tauern

ZELL AM SEE
Mayer's
Schloss Prielau, Hofmannsthalstrasse; tel: 06542-729 110; www.schloss-prielau.at; €€€; daily 6–10pm
Dine like royalty in this castle. The restaurant has earnt two Michelin stars under chef Andreas Mayer and specialises in modern Austrian dishes – there is a big emphasis on local ingredients – arranged in a series of different menus. Some of the dining rooms are non-smoking; reservations are highly recommended. The chef also runs cooking courses for those who are keen.

Zum Hirschenwirt
Dreifaltigkeitsgasse 1; tel: 06542-7740; www.biowirtshaus.at; €€; daily 11.30am–midnight, kitchen closes 10.30pm
This is an excellent longstanding restaurant that has a light touch with the local specialities. Dishes change throughout the year to take account of seasonal ingredients; if you are lucky, the mushrooms are particularly good here.

115

Shopping

Salzburg is starting to make its mark as an upmarket shopping destination. The tiny streets of the Altstadt hide big-name designer shops and smaller boutiques with some elegant and some quirky designs. If you take a shine to the local dress, then there are plenty of opportunities to acquire a pair of *Lederhosen* or a *Dirndl*. More shops lie across the river in the New Town, and if you are feeling in need of the Euro-mall experience then look no further than the huge Europark out near the airport. The obvious present to take home, however, must be some of the city's *Mozartkugeln*.

Shopping Areas

The major shopping area in the centre of the city is around Getreidegasse and, especially, in the small passages that run between this road and Universitätsplatz on one side and Griesgasse on the other. This is the location for up-market boutiques and shops selling Salzburger *Tracht*.

A large part of the right bank of the River Salzach is occupied by a pedestrianised zone. This area incorporates Linzergasse, Bergstrasse, Priesterhausgasse, Dreifaltigkeitsgasse and Steingasse, which between them house some of the city's best shopping opportunities. Out-of-towners can approach the zone by bus 4 along Schallmooser Hauptstrasse to the north or bus 27 along Schwarzstrasse.

Europark

Europastrasse 1; tel: 0662 442 0210; www.europark.at; Mon–Thur 9am–7.30pm, Fri 9am–9pm, Sat 9am–6pm; bus: 20, S-bahn: S3; map p.134 C3
Twenty minutes out of the town centre by public trans-

Above: browsing the *Tracht* on Getreidegasse.

port, Europark is where all the cultural ambivalences of post-imperial Austria succumb to the demands of contemporary capitalism. In this ultra-modern shopping mall, incongruously still within view of those beautiful mountains, you can shop in stores identical to their siblings the world over, buy generic fast food from workers in T-shirts and baseball caps, and entirely forget which continent, let alone

country, you are visiting… On a more positive note, there are a number of contemporary clothing stores congregated here which are useful for those on a fashion mission.

Fashion

Einfach Schön
Imbergstrasse 22; map p.133 D3 and Schwartzstrasse 4, bei Staatsbrücke;map p.132 C3 Mon–Fri 10am–6pm, Sat 10am–1pm
These are two mid-price boutiques selling a good range of womens' fashion.

Ellie Fashion
Goldgasse 6; www.elliefashion.com; Mon–Sat 10am–6pm; map p.132 C3
This is a great boutique selling sexy and fashionalbe clothes from a hand-picked range of designers.

Madl
Getreidegasse 13/Universitätsplatz 12; www.madlsalzburg.at; Tue–Fri 10am–5.30pm, Sat 10am–5pm; map p.132 B3
One of the best places to go for made-to-measure evening clothes and *Tracht*. The details on the clothes can be exquisite.

Tracht

Salzburg is famous for its *Tracht* (Austrian traditional dress; *Lederhosen* and *Dirndl*). The city's museums have an excellent collection of local costume (once part of the now-closed Trachten Sammlung). The women's clothes especially are very flattering, *Lederhosen* might need a bit more courage to get away with on your local high street. However, if you feel the need to recreate your own Alpine idyll when you get home, or are looking for the perfect costume for that 'Sing-a-long-a-*Sound of Music*', you have come to the right place.

Lanz
Schwarzstrasse 4; www.lanz trachten.at; Mon–Fri 9am–6pm, Sat 9am–5pm; map p.132 C3
Some of the very best, in top-quality fabrics.

Salzberger Heimatwerk
Residenzplatz 9; www.sbg. heimatwerk.at; Mon–Sat 9am– 6pm; map p.132 C3
High quality and with an impressive pedigree.

Trachten Stassny
Getreidegasse 35; www.stassny. at; Mon–Fri 9.30am– 6pm, Sat 9.30am–5pm; map p.132 B3
Seriously good clothing; pieces are updated each season.

Shopping for kitsch souvenirs should not be much of a problem in Salzbug as there is in the main tourist areas an inordinate amount on display, most if it branded with a picture of Mozart. Perhaps the best option is a box of *Mozartkugel*, the chocolate and marzipan sweet for which the city is well-known *(see also Food and Drink, p.75)*.

Misc.Fashion
Mozartplatz 5; Mon–Sat 10am–5pm; www.misc-fash ion.at; map p.133 C3
This new boutique specialises in women's fashion from Scandinavian designers; expect lots of clean, feminine lines and neutral colours.

Lingerie and Hosiery
Rositta
Alter Markt 15; www.rositta.at; Mon–Fri 9.30am–6pm, Sat 9.30am–5pm; map p.132 C3
Top lingerie from La Perla and Féraud as well as beautiful blouses.

Veronika-Unschuldige Dessous
Getreidegasse 3;

www.unschuldige-dessous.at; Mon–Fri 10am–6.30pm, Sat 10am–5pm; map p.132 C3
Sexy silk undies and fashionable swimwear.

Wolford
Kranzlmarkt 5; www.wolford. com; map p.132 C3
High quality Austrian hosiery and underwear.

Shoes and Accessories
Mia Shoes
Rathausplatz 1; www.miashoes.at; Mon–Sat 9am– 6.30pm, Sat 9am–6pm; map p.132 C3
Funky and stylish mid-priced shoes and accessories.

Below: a Mozart ball or two?

Spas

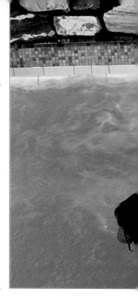

Spa therapy has a long and global history, viewed with wildly fluctuating levels of interest and respect by practitioners, the medical community and the wider public. Austrian spas, and above all those which exploit the mineral-rich waters of the Salzkammergut, have won a significant reputation among today's 'health tourists', who seek to tend body and soul during their leisure travels. Long a centre for taking the 'healing waters', the province of Salzburg has a number of spas where you can relax and unwind, and, who knows, it might even be good for your health.

Paracelsus

One Salzburg figure, Philip von Hohenheim (1493–1541), who took the name Paracelsus in his work as a travelling healer and pioneer of toxicology, was a particularly important contributor to the discipline of spa therapy via the schools of medical thought which followed in the trail he blazed. Paracelsus' empirical approach, rejecting much of classical authority, created a spa culture out of the Alps which was distinctive from that developed principally by Italian Renaissance doctors on the basis of recovered texts from the ancient Greeks and Romans.

Spa Mania

By the 19th century, the use of mineral waters in developments built around hotels and guesthouses had spread across Europe. Spas had become popular in the treatment of work-related injuries and in the small town of Bad Ischl, one Dr Josef Götz began prescribing the waters to treat gout and rheumatism in local miners.

At the northern boundary of the Mirabell Gardens in Salzburg's New Town is the public **Paracelsus Spa** (www.paracelsusbad.at). Since 1968 Salzburg has been an officially recognised spa town because of the supposed healing properties of its mud, brine and mineral water.

This led to a curiosity about the method among Habsburg court physicians, and after Archduchess Sophie's successful spa treatments for infertility in the 1820s, 'spa mania' hit the Austro-Hungarian territories. Austria quickly became a principal player in a network of spa facilities, stretching across Britain, Belgium and the German-speaking lands, which courted the elite of the continent and combined therapeutic spa treatments in ostentatious settings with entertainment including theatres, casinos and well-furnished promenades.

The spa resorts became popular among artists and thinkers as well as the vacation spots of the European elite, their devotion to peace and leisure seen as inspirational for creative work.

Today's Salzburger spas, centuries distant from Paracelsus, share their therapeutic approaches with their sister institutions the world over. They owe more to Ayurveda or alternative therapies than Renaissance alchemy, but they remain internationally distinctive in their high standards which derive from the traditions of imperial tourism.

The Salzkammergut

The Kaisertherme

Vogelhuberstrasse 10, 4820 Bad Ischl; tel: 06132-2040; www.kaisertherme.at; daily 9am–midnight; entrance charge; map p.137 D2
Appropriately enough, Bad Ischl's Kaisertherme are among the most affordable and renowned of Austrian spa waters. These, the pre-eminent baths of the Salzkammergut, were favoured by the emperor himself. The Kaisertherme is considered Austria's leading

Left: baths at Bad Gastein.

Other Spas

The spa at St Georgen im Attergau's **Hotel Winzer** provides a comprehensive range of treatments, but specialises in 'New-Age' therapies. The modern facilities and décor reflect the owners' level of investment in the property. The holistic approach means that *shiatsu*, *ayurveda*, *reiki* and massage are complemented not only by aqua-gym and yoga classes but also a number of saunas, rest rooms designed around different philosophies, including *feng shui*, and healthy menus.

Other significant spa centres include Gmunden's **Lacus Felix** facility on the Traunsee, which focusses on healing the mind as much as the body (tel: 07612-77961; www.lacus-felix.at); and **Schloss Mondsee**, which hosts the Shenmen-Therapie Centre, offering a mix of Chinese and Western therapies.
SEE ALSO HOTELS, P.86

Below: the entrance to a Bad Gastein spa.

Paracelsus noted the curative properties of the waters at Bad Gastein in his lifetime, but was unable to explain them. It took Marie Curie's discovery of radium to solve the 5,000-year-old riddle of the 'miracle cures'.

spa for those with respiratory conditions. Within the spa complex, one may swim in the mineral-rich water both in and out of doors, using two pools connected by a swimmable passage. There are also Jacuzzi facilities.

For travellers on a tight budget, or the merely curious, a cheap offer at the Kaisertherme can usually be found for a 3-hour session with access to the spa waters, though the refundable deposit almost doubles the amount to be paid up front. This deposit gives you the key to a secure individual changing room which doubles as a locker.

Families may use larger shared changing rooms, but these cannot be used to store valuables. The spa is mostly used by retired Austrians or young families; children will love the pool but childless travellers may find that 3 hours is a little too long. There is a reasonable café beyond the changing rooms, to be entered in swimwear. Those truly devoted to the cult of body beautiful can even down a mug of the spa waters.

The Salzach and High Tauern

The Alpentherme
Senator-Wilhelm-Wifling-Platz 1, 5630 Bad Hofgastein; tel: 06432-829 3300; www. alpentherme.com; Thur–Sat 9am–10pm, Sun–Wed 9am–9pm; entrance charge
Another major spa complex is the Alpentherme at Bad Gastein. Here a wide range of innovate spa and pool installation offer rest, relaxation and therapy, but also high-adrenalin activities for children of all ages (the 'Black Hole Rafting' ride being a particular thriller). There are sports facilities too, with a wide range of special offers and activity combinations available.

Sport

Salzburg Province is a paradise for anyone looking for an active holiday. The region is one of the best skiing areas in the world and during the winter is popular with skiers from all over Europe. The area's beautiful mountains, lakes and rivers are a draw for mountaineers, climbers and walkers, as well as cyclists – both on and off road – and for those who enjoy rafting, canoeing and diving in the clear waters of the Salzkammergut. These activities do not have to be strenuous or for the intrepid, and much of the beautiful countryside can be seen from gentle walks on easy footpaths.

Walking and Climbing

The Salzburg region offers some of the finest walking and climbing in the eastern Alps. The highest peaks, the Grossvenediger and the Grossglockner – the latter actually lies in Carinthia – are accessible only to trained climbers with mountaineering experience. The mountains surrounding Salzburg, however, attract many less experienced climbers.

For the most basic of mountain walks you need proper boots and waterproofs. For more ambitious tours it is well worth engaging the services of a trained mountain guide. Guided tours of varying difficulty lasting for several days are offered in the Saalach Valley and conducted walks are offered in the West Dachstein region. The highlight is a two-day tour of the glaciers on the Dachstein. A trekking guide covering the Tennengau holiday region is available locally. Starting from St Martin, ambitious mountain walkers can follow the Gosau Gorge across the Postalm

Above: standing on the highest suspension bridge in Europe, located atop Stubnerkogel, in Gastein valle.

and the Osterhorn group to Puch in the Salzach Valley. In the High Tauern National Park, the park rangers also lead mountain walks.

Useful publications include the Arno Weg Guidebook, covering the 1,200km (745 miles) of Salzburg's borders, and the Salzburg Hiking Atlas, featuring 10 trekking tours. Both publications are available from the regional tourist board. A new trail has recently been inaugurated: the 803-km (499-mile) Jacob's Trail pilgrims' route. This follows the Danube in one direction; in the other it follows the Austrian-German border before crossing the Salzkammergut and arriving in Salzburg.

SEE ALSO WALKS, P.128

LEARNING TO CLIMB

Climbing is taught in many mountaineering schools with the rock faces popular as practice walls. For more information and advice contact the Salzburg section of the Österreichischer Alpenverein (Nonntaler Hauptstrasse 86; tel: 0662-822 692; www.alpenverein. or.at). The Austrian Mountain Guides' Association is another good source of information (www.bergfuehrer.at).

Austria's mountaineering schools also offer courses in rock climbing. Rock climbers are drawn to the tricky faces in one of Austria's increasing number of climbing parks (one of the best known is in Bad Ischl in the Salzkammergut). Most routes are in the limestone Alps, in the Gastein Valley or in the Salzkammergut.

Left: skiing at Flachau, not too far from Salzburg.

Kaprun (www.tauerntouristik.at) is the second most important centre of the European Sports Region after Zell am See. It offers facilities for 30 different sports disciplines on the ground, in the air and under water. In spite of the magnificence of the surrounding mountains, tourism is a relatively recent addition to the valley of the Kapruner Ache. The stream of visitors which began to arrive during the 1950s also encouraged the development of the Kitzstein-horn (3,200m/10,499ft) into an all-year skiing area.

Skiing

Salzburg is a well-located city for skiing and snow-boarding, with some of the best slopes in the world within relatively easy reach. The province has hosted the Alpine Skiing World Championships, as well as ski jumping and snowboarding competitions. Whether you are an absolute beginner or an experienced skier, you will find a slope to suit your needs. Most of the major ski resorts are to the south of Salzburg, the nearest being just 20 minutes away and the best of them between 45 and 90 minutes from the city. The resorts offer a wide choice of accommodation, including slope-side Alpine cabins, as well as numerous shops, restaurants, banks and a good nightlife. Off-piste skiing, cross-country, ice-skating, tobogganing and night skiing are just some of the additional activities you can do. Among the ski areas within comfortable travelling distance of Salzburg are Flachau, Obertauern, Badgastein, Zell Am See and Saalbach-Hinterglemm.

The best way to get to the resorts from Salzburg is by train, leaving early in the morning. The information desk at the railway station will be able to advise you about the best way to get to your destination. If you are staying in Salzburg during the winter season and would like to go skiing for just one or two days, during the winter season there are special bus services for skiers, sometimes operated for free (see www.postbus.at for details).

One day you might be in Flachau, the next in Kitzbühel, but every evening you can be back in Salzburg.

SKI AREAS
Amadé Sports World

Consists of the three-valley ski areas Flachau–Wagrain–St Johann and Zauchensee–Flachauwinkel–Kleinarl, as well as the Altenmarkt–Radstadt and Filzmoos–Neuberg ski areas, and the Eben lifts; a total of 320km (199 miles) of pistes with 120 lifts and 220km (137 miles) of cross-country tracks.

Below: rafting has become a popular activity in the Salzach Valley.

Left: diving in the clear waters of the Salzkammergut.

machines use chemicals and deplete water supplies (the increased snow melt also heightens erosion); there is a huge amount of littering which remains for years on the slopes; flying adds greatly to global warming; and, while some money does enter the local economy the jobs created are temporary and many are taken by itinerant workers rather than locals. There is also a trend for rich foreigners to buy up chalets, which would otherwise have been used by local people, that are only in use during the ski season. Last but not least, ski lifts litter the mountain slopes and impact greatly on the visual beauty of the area.

A number of organisations can help you book through responsible tour operators, which aim to limit their impact on the environment (see: www.responsible travel.com; www.tourismconcern. org.uk; and www.skiclub.co.uk). Certain measures are a matter of common sense: don't fly but take the train to the ski area you are staying in; avoid resorts that use snow machines; don't throw litter (and pick up any you see); don't ski off-piste; and stay and eat in locally owned and staffed hotels and restaurants.

One of the few tourist activities which may directly endanger the environment is scuba diving in the region's many lakes. This is often prohibited for set months of the year in order to protect wildlife; always take personal responsibility for ensuring that your dives take place during the permitted season.

'Europe' Ski Region Kaprun–Zell am See
including Schmittenhöhe and Kitzensteinhorn with 130km (81 miles) of pistes, 54 lifts and 300km (186 miles) of cross-country tracks.

Gastein Valley–Grossarltal
170km (106 miles) of pistes with 53 lifts and 150km (93 miles) of cross-country tracks.

Hochkönig Ski area and Ski Maria Alm–Saalfelden
160km (99 miles) of pistes with 47 lifts and 200km (124 miles) of cross-country tracks.

Lungau ski region
320km (199 miles) of pistes, 40 lifts and 320km (199 miles) of cross-country tracks.

Obertauern
150km (93 miles) of pistes, a total of 26 lifts, 18km (11 miles) of cross-country tracks.

Postalm
11km (7 miles) of pistes, 9 draglifts, 20km (12 miles) of cross-country tracks.

Saalbach–Hinterglemm– Leogang Ski area
200km (124 miles) of pistes, a total of 60 lifts and 95km (59 miles) cross-country tracks.

Ski area West Dachstein/Tennengau
Includes Abtenau, St Martin, Annaberg and Russbach, with 195km (121 miles) of pistes, a total of 61 lifts and 260km (161 miles) of cross-country tracks.

ENVIRONMENTAL IMPACTS
Skiing is in danger of becoming a victim of its own popularity and visitors should be aware of its impact on the mountain environment. Slopes are artifically graded; ski edges destroy underlying flora (which leads to both a degradation of the biodiversity and increases erosion); wildife is disturbed by the huge influx of visitors; resorts are developing to ever higher altitudes and environments become increasingly fragile the higher you go; snow

---

Canoeing and Rafting

Wild-water sports, including river-rafting in large rubber dinghies take place on the Salzach (starting from Zell am See, Krimml, Taxenbach, Schwarzach and St Johann im Pongau), on the Salzach and the Lammer (starting from Abtenau, Golling, Scheffau, Bischofshofen,

Werfen and Kuchl), on the Saalach (starting from Lofer, Unken, Saalbach-Hinter-glemm and Saalbach), on the Mur (starting from Tamsweg, Vordertullnberg, and Mauterndorf) and in the Salzkammergut (Bad Gois-ern, Bad Ischl, Obertraun, Ebensee, Hallstatt and St Wolfgang).

Cycling and Mountain Biking

There are numerous cycle hire places throughout the region that offer mountain bikes. Together, with the tourist authority, they also provide information concern-ing places where mountain bikes are welcome and where, in the interests of the protection of plant and ani-mal life, they are not.

The **Tauern Cycle Path**, which is clearly marked throughout its entire length, leads along some 300km (186 miles) of cycle-tracks and quiet roads through a wide variety of landscapes. It winds through the Krimml Waterfalls in the High Tauern National Park to the Pongau and the Tennengau on to Salzburg, continuing through the gently undulat-ing countryside of the Alpine foothills to Passau and beyond. The route follows the downhill course of the Salzach, so there are no uphill sections. (The Tauern Cycle Path guide can be bought at bookstores or from the Salzburg Regional Tourist Authority.)

The Pinzgau section of the Saalach Valley also offers keen cyclists plenty of variety, from easy terrain to circuits for mountain cyclists and a sprint parcours for mountain bikers. The sug-gested routes for the Lun-gau range from the Mur

Valley to challenging moun-tain tours.

Cycle tours can also be planned through the Ten-nengau section of the Salzach Valley, through the gently rolling hills and moor-land of the Alpine foothills around Salzburg, in the Amadé Sports World in Salzburg, in the Pongau and in the Europe Sports Region around Zell am See and Kaprun.

Sailing and Wind Surfing

The Attersee, Wolfgangsee (the largest and deepest of the lakes) and Mondsee are all great for sailing and surf-ing, as are the smaller Fuschlsee, Mattsee, Obertrumer See, Wallersee, Irrsee, Grundlsee and Zeller See. You can rent sailing boats and windsurfing boards at all these lakes.

Swimming

Salzburg has a number of outdoor swimming pools, which are well maintained and very clean. The outdoor pools are at the following locations: Leopoldskron (bus 15); Volksgarten (bus 6, 7); and Alpenstrasse (bus 3, 5, 8). There is also an indoor swimming pool in the city centre at Paracelsus Bad und Kurhaus, Auerspergstrasse 2.

For the Alpine lakes, with crystal-clear water and breathtaking views, catch a Post Bus from the railway station or Mirabellplatz. If you want to sunbathe or swim, then follow the signs to *Freibad*. The new **Alpentherme** water park in Gastein has everything from saunas and slides to beauti-ful outdoor pools with a panoramic view of the Alps. SEE ALSO SPAS, P.119

Below: cycling the Hochalpenstrasse is quite a challenge.

Transport

Salzburg is well-connected with surrounding areas (less than 2 hours from Munich) and a fast and efficient train service will get you there from the UK. There are also several daily flights from Britain to Wolfgang Amadeus Airport from where it is only 30 minutes into the city centre. If you do decide to fly rather than take the train then consider 'off-setting' the carbon from your flight (www.jpmorganclimatecare.com). Once you have arrived then you can take advantage of Salzburg's excellent public transport, both in the city and across the region, though the city itself is eminently walkable.

Getting There

BY RAIL

On the international railway network, Salzburg lies on both the north–south axis (Germany–Italy–Balkan countries) and the east–west axis (France–Switzerland–Hungary), so it is easily and quickly reached from any direction (for information on any of these see www.seat61.com or www.raileurope.co.uk).

From London there are two options, both via Munich. The first goes via Paris (take the Eurostar from St Pancras; www.eurostar.com), connecting with the DB *Nachtzug* sleeper service from the Gare de l'Est to München arriving early in the morning (www.nachtzug reise.de) and take the next train to Salzburg (there is a regular service taking just under 2 hours). Alternatively, take the early Eurostar to Brussels and connect for Köln where you can pick up the ICE train (www.bahn.de) to München in time for the last departure for Salzburg, or stay overnight and take the train the next morning.

Above: the funicular railway up to Salzburg's fortress.

The Austrian railways (www.oebb.at) are very efficient and clean. If you are travelling on from Salzburg, the train from Vienna to Salzburg takes about 3 hours. Salzburg Hauptbahnhof (Central Railway Station) is about 15 mins walk from the city centre though buses leave from outside to most destinations.

BY AIR

From the UK there are a number of flights to Salzburg (www.salzburg-airport.com).

Coach tours are available to many of the major sights in the region, including the Salzkammergut, Berchtesgaden and the Eisriesenwelt caves, not forgetting the ever-popular Sound of Music Tour (Salzburg Panorama Tours; 2 Schrannengasse; tel: 0662-883 2110; www.panoramatours.com). River tours are also a popular way to get a view of the city, boats depart from Makartsteg in the Altstadt and go as far as Hellbrunn (Stadt Schiff-Fahrt; Makartsteg; tel: 0662-825 858; www.salzburgschifffahrt.at).

British Airways flies four times a week from Gatwick (www.ba.com) and Ryanair (www.ryanair.com) four times a week from Stansted. In addition Flybe (www.flybe.com) has one flight a week from Southampton. There are also charter flights on Thomson (www.thomsonfly. com) and BMI (www.flybmi.com) from regional airports, and Air Berlin (www. airberlin.com) has a winter-only service from Stansted.

The airport lies between the Maxglan district of town

city, including Oberndorf and Maria Plain (see www.salzburg-ag.at). The local railway network is currently being expanded and the Hauptbahnhof is due for a complete revamp. Progress on the new S-bahn stops and network in and around Salzburg can be followed at www.s-bahn-salzburg.at.

Regional Services

Austrian Railways (www.oebb.at) also has services across the province. Three important railway lines cross the Salzburg region: Salzburg– Zell am See–Saalfelden– Kitzbühel; Salzburg–Gasteiner Tal–Villach; and Salzburg–Radstadt–Graz. A narrow-gauge railway serves the Vöcklamarkt– Attersee and Tamsweg–Unzmarkt sections, as well as Zell am See–Krimml.

BICYCLE HIRE

Top Bike Salzburg
Salzburg Hauptbahnhof and Staatsbrücke; tel: 0676-476 7259; www.topbike.at; map p.132 C3
Bicycles can be hired for the day (€15) from the railway station and besides the Staatsbrücke.

and the suburb of Himmelreich, about 4km (2.5 miles) from the town centre. The airport is linked with the town centre by means of a shuttle bus service as well as by bus no. 2.

ENTRY

EU nationals as well as visitors from many other countries, including the US, Canada, Australia and New Zealand, do not require a visa for Austria. Visas are still required by nationals of some Commonwealth countries.

Getting Around

BY BUS

Salzburg has a very efficient public transport system. The bus information office on Mirabellplatz (see www. salzburg-ag.at). It is possible to buy tickets from the driver when getting on the bus and from the machines at some of the main bus stops, but it is cheaper to buy your tickets in advance. They are available from tobacconists (all marked with the Austria Tabak sign). You can buy blocks of five

single tickets, 24-hour tickets or weekly tickets.

Post buses (www.postbus.at) serve the outlying districts and the wider region and go to many places that cannot be reached by train. Timetables can be found at the railway station. You need to pay the driver when getting on the bus. Tickets cannot be bought in advance.

BY RAIL

Lokalbahn

This commuter-train route currently serves many destinations to the north of the

Below: a bicycle is a good way to explore both the city and region.

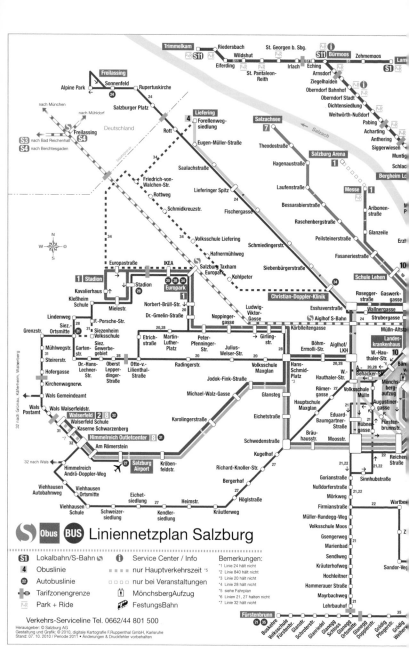

Verkehrs-Serviceline Tel. 0662/44 801 500

Herausgeber: © Salzburg AG
Gestaltung und Grafik: © 2010, digitale Kartografie F.Ruppenthal GmbH, Karlsruhe
Stand: 07. 10. 2010 / Periode 2011 · Änderungen & Druckfehler vorbehalten

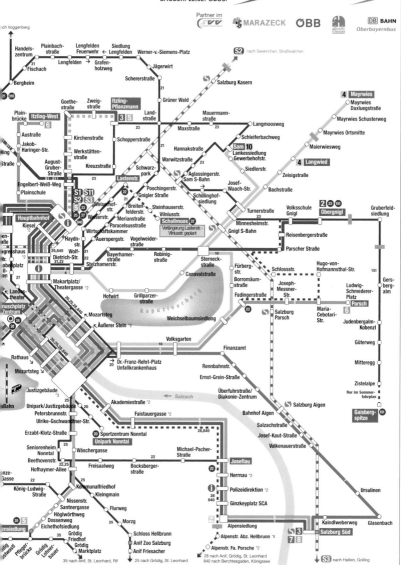

Walks

The walks described below are generally easy, well within the capabilities of most visitors and provided with places to stop and take refreshment. The full-day excursion up the Untersberg, however, is a little different. This is very rewarding with wonderful views, but you will need to start early, be fit with a good head for heights and be well-equipped as the weather can be treacherous and changes very quickly. The most useful map, for this and other walks in the immediate mountains, is the Kompass Wander- und Bikekarte 017: Salzburg und Umgebung (1:35,000), easily found in bookshops in the city.

The Kapuzinerberg

This 636m (2,087ft) mountain, the icon and highlight of Salzburg's right bank, offers a haven for locals, tourists and woodland wildlife alike. Walking up from the Linzergasse to the Chapel of St John is a matter of five minutes' undemanding ascent, offering fine views of the city. From here, those with sufficient energy can ascend still further to the summit, which shows off Salzburg to its best.

The view to the north of the Kapuzinerberg is rather mundane, consisting of retail parks and freight railway lines, but the view of the impossibly close mountains to the south is awe inspiring. During Nazi rule, it had been intended to exploit the power of this view by crowning the peak with a regional headquarters for government, sports and culture, thankfully never built, dominating the landscape for miles around.

The walk up the Kapuzinerberg, steep in places, lasts 1½–2 hours for the complete circuit, although 30 minutes will suffice by sticking to the most direct, signposted paths. Away from these trails, the going can be gravelly and treacherous, with the steps that have been cut worn to unevenness. Tree felling and groundskeeping procedures sometimes make walking difficult and you must also give way to the occasional passing tractor. Wear sensible shoes and take a drink, although the Wirtshaus at the summit provides excellent refreshment.

Below: a good pair of boots is essential.

Krimml Falls

For the average walker, the walk from the car park near the waterfalls to above the third and highest sill will take approximately 2 hours. If you are an experienced walker you can continue for another hour through the valley of the Krimmler Ache to the Krimmler Tauernhaus (1,620m/5,315ft; with restaurant), or even further on to the end of the valley at the edge of the glacier of the Krimmler Kees (2,000m/ 6,562ft; another 2½ hours). where you are unlikely to meet many other walkers.

The Untersberg

Take the 21 bus to Glanegg Ortsmitte. This will drop you at a T-junction, turn right along the road and carry straight on after it turns sharp left. This brings you to the car park at the start of the footpath. Walk up along the track and where it forks beside the stream take the left hand path (signposted **Dopplersteig**); from here red flashes of paint on the rocks will help you navigate. The right hand path, the Rupertiweg, will also bring you

Left: the Untersberg.

is so steep that a shaft has had to be cut through the rock. Where the steps finish a path leads across the bottom of the crags with glorious views of the mountains to the south. At about 4½–5 hours you reach the Toni-Lenz-Hütte, a useful stopping place for some refreshment.

Leaving the hut, the path winds steeply down, at first through low bushes and then entering the forest. After a while it becomes a wide forest track and at about 6½–7 hours you reach the road at the bottom, with a bus stop (on the opposite side) where you can catch a bus to Salzburg.

The Wolfgangsee

St Wolfgang and its rival St Gilgen are connected by regular ferry services, but you might consider walking the fringe of the lake, a journey of some 4 hours which passes through Reid, Furberg and the minor Mt Falkenstein going in an east to west direction. Tourist offices of the region can supply route maps which also indicate the *Sehenswürdigkeiten*, or 'things worth seeing', which populate the trail.

Below: descending the Untersberg to the Toni-Lenz-Hütte.

> The Untersberg is said to be home to mythical creatures, including dwarfs, giants and wild women, and has given rise to a number of legends. The emperor Karl the Great is said to be asleep in a cavern under the mountain and when the ravens that circle the summit disappear he will rise and fight the battle of good against evil.

to the summit but is easier and less spectacular.

The path begins to climb steeply through the trees, passing memorials to local climbers. Take care on this initial section as it is damp and slippery and it would be easy to fall. After a short while the gradient eases and for a while it is a pleasant walk up through the forest.

A series of steep stairways brings you up to the meadow below summit crags. Cross this, taking the right hand path to the foot of a *Klettersteig* (roped stairway; 1–1½ hours). Although not exposed enough to merit the use of specialist equipment, this is very steep and the feeling of

height is more than enough to concentrate the mind. Move carefully and take your time.

At the top you reach the limestone summit plateau and are rewarded with fabulous views. The next section, which feels a little cruel on your calves, leads up through bushes to the **Zeppezauer Haus** mountain hut (1,663m/5,456ft, 2–2½ hours) where you can get food and drinks.

Make now for the summit itself, past the cable car station at Geiereck (1,805m/5,922ft) to the **Salzburger Hochthron** (1,853m/6,078ft). The views are stupendous, especially of the elegant peak of the Watzmann. The path continues on and you soon leave the crowds behind. After 30 minutes it dips steeply to a col between the Untersberg and the Berchtesgadener peaks ahead.

Take the path to the left, signposted to the Toni-Lenz-Hütte. You are now in Germany and very quickly you reach the top of another *Klettersteig*, a series of ladders leading down the side of the mountain. In places this

Atlas

The following atlas of greater Salzburg makes it easy to find the attractions listed in the A–Z section. A selective index to streets and sights will help you find other locations throughout the region.

Map Legend

Railway		Tourist information	
Pedestrian area		Bus station	
Notable building		Sight of interest	
Park		Funicular railway/ Cable car	
Hotel		Cathedral / church	
Urban area		Summit	
Non urban area		Viewpoint	
Cemetery		Hospital	
National park		Airport	
National boundary		Castle	
Provincial boundary		Cave	
Tunnel		Monastery	

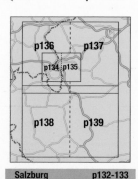

p136	p137
p134	p135
p138	p139

Salzburg	p132-133

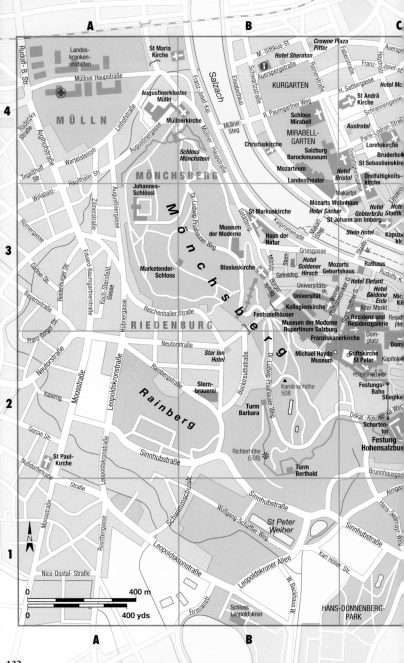

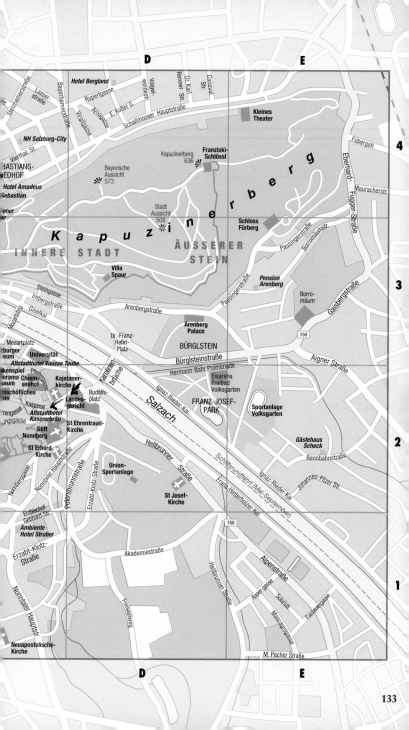

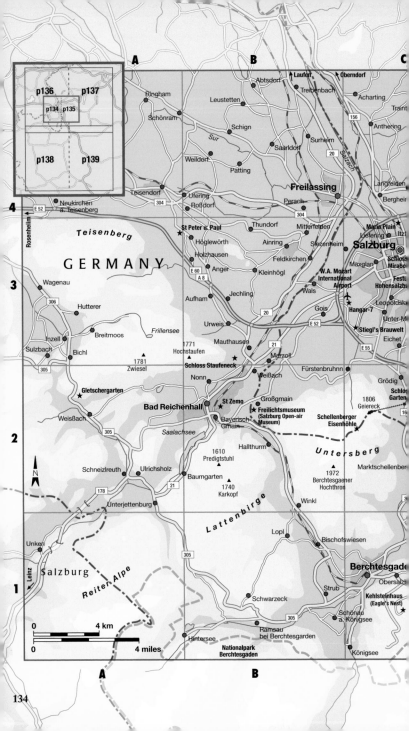

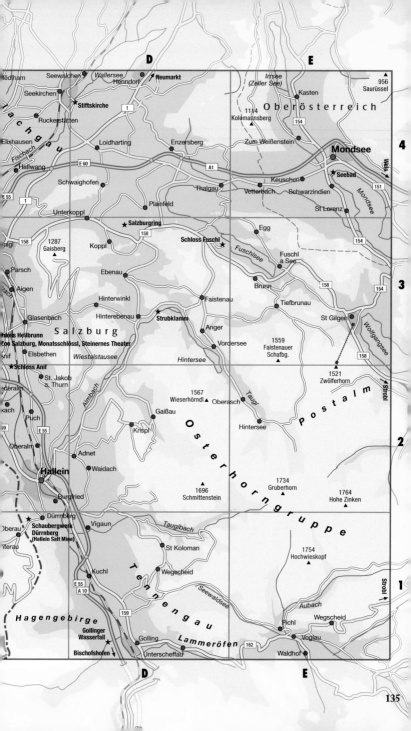

Seewalchen *Wallersee* Henndorf **Neumarkt**

Fedham

Seekirchen

★ **Stiftskirche**

Ruckerstätten

Elixhausen

Fischach

Hallwang

E 60

E 55

1

Loidharting

Schwaighofen

Plainfeld

Unterkoppl

158

1287
Gaisberg ▲

★ **Salzburgring**
158

Koppl

Ebenau

Hinterwinkl

Hinterebenau

★ **Strubklamm**

S a l z b u r g

Glasenbach

Schloss Hellbrunn
Zoo Salzburg, Monatsschlössl, Steinernes Theater

Parsch

Aigen

Elsbethen

★ **Schloss Anif**

St. Jakob
a. Thurn

deralm

Puch

E 55

59

Oberalm

Adnet

Waidach

Hallein

Burgfried

Dürrnberg

**Schaubergwerk
Dürrnberg
(Hallein Salt Mine)**

Oberau

nterau

H a g e n g e b i r g e

**Gollinger
Wasserfall** ★

Bischofshofen ↓

Vigaun

Kuchl

E 55
A 10

159

T e n n e n g a u

Golling

Unterscheffau

D

*Irrsee
(Zeller See)*

Kasten

▲ 956
Saurüssel

O b e r ö s t e r r e i c h

1114 ▲
Kolomannsberg

154

Zum Weißenstein

Mondsee

Wels

151

Enzersberg

A1

Thalgau

Keuschen

★ **Seebad**

Vetterbach

Schwarzindien

Mondsee

St Lorenz

154

Egg

Schloss Fuschl

Fuschlsee

Fuschl
a See

158

154

Brunn

Tiefbrunau

St Gilgen

Wolfgangsee

Faistenau

Anger

Vordersee

1559
Faistenauer
Schafbg. ▲

1521
Zwölferhorn

158

Strobl

Hintersee

1567
Wieserhörndl ▲

Oberasch

Taugl

Hintersee

Gaißau

Krispl

O s t e r h o r n g r u p p e

P o s t a l m

1696
Schmittenstein ▲

1734
Gruberhorn ▲

1764
Hohe Zinken ▲

Tauglbach

St Koloman

Wegscheid

1754
Hochwieskopf ▲

Seewaldsee

L a m m e r ö f e n

162

Pichl

Aubach

Wegscheid

Voglau

Waldhof

Strobl

E

135

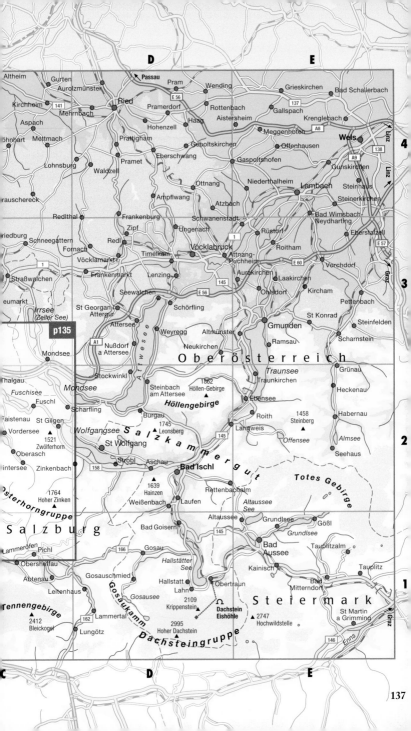

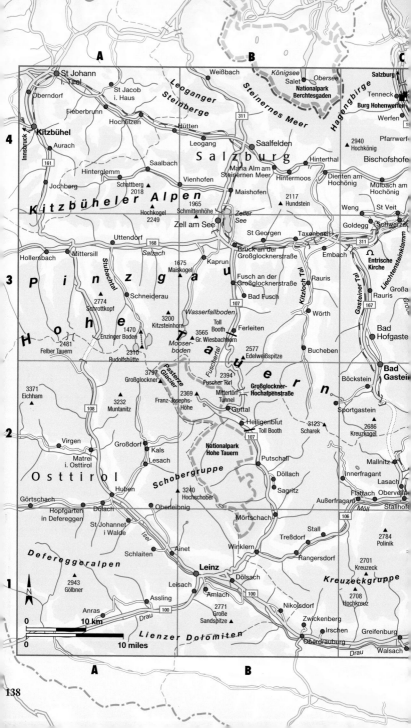

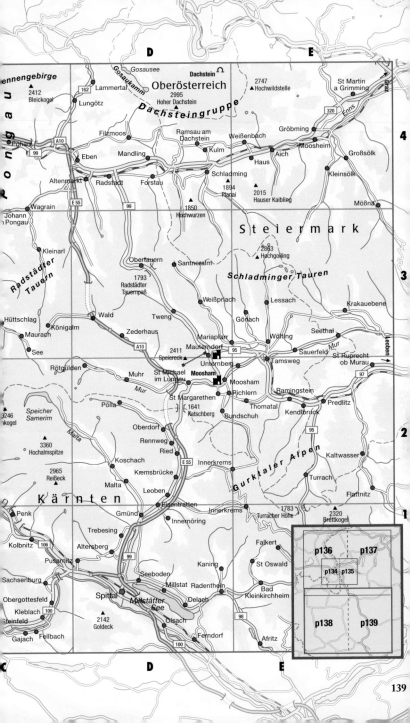

141

Index

Insight Smart Guide: Salzburg
Compiled and updated by: **Maria Lord**
and **Matthew Finch**
Proofread and indexed by: **Penny Phenix**
Photography by: All Pictures © **APA/
Mockford-Bonetti** except: **4 Corners** 87,
120-121; **Alamy** 86, 124–5; **AKG** 78TL,
79TL, 79MR; **Bridgeman** 78M; **Allie
Caulfield** 42; **Corbis** 15, 54, 55, 66–7,
68–9, 72–3, 72B, 73B, 78B, 79TR, 79B;
Bortes Christian 118/119; **Fotolia** 77TR,
102/121; **Getty** 68–9, 79MR, 91, 92–3,
92B, 104–5; **Granthan** 124/125; **Istock-
photo** 120; **Lebrecht** 70–1, 70L, 70R,
90, 97, 104, 105; **Maria Lord** 42, 120,
124; **This is Bossi** 95; **ZeHawk** 124

Picture Manager: **Steven Lawerence**
Maps: **APA Cartography Dept, Tom
Coulson, Encompass Graphics Ltd**
Series Editor: **Sarah Sweeney**

Second Edition 2011, First Edition 2008
©2011 Apa Publications (UK) Limited
Printed by CTPS-China
Worldwide distribution enquiries:
APA Publications GmbH & Co Verlag KG
(Singapore branch); 7030 Ang Mo Kio Ave 5,
08-65 Northstar @ AMK, Singapore
569880; email: apasin@singnet.com.sg
Distributed in the UK and Ireland by:
GeoCenter International Ltd; Meridian House,
Churchill Way West, Basingstoke, Hampshire,
RG21 6YR; email: sales@geocenter.co.uk
Distributed in the United States by:
Ingram Publisher Services
One Ingram Blvd, PO Box 3006, La Vergne,
TN 37086-1986; email: customer.
service@ingrampublisherservices.com
Distributed in Australia by:
Universal Publishers; PO Box 307,
St. Leonards, NSW 1590; email:
sales@universalpublishers.com.au

Distributed in New Zealand by:
Hema Maps New Zealand Ltd (HNZ); Unit 2,
10 Cryers Road, East Tamaki, Auckland
2013; email: sales.hema@clear.net.nz
Contacting the Editors
We would appreciate it if readers would alert us
to errors or outdated information by writing to:
Apa Publications, PO Box 7910, London SE1
1WE, UK; fax: (44 20) 7403 0290;
email: insight@apaguide.co.uk
No part of this book may be reproduced,
stored in a retrieval system or transmitted in
any form or by any means (electronic,
mechanical, photocopying, recording or
otherwise), without prior written permission of
Apa Publications. Brief text quotations with
use of photographs are exempted for book
review purposes only. Information has been
obtained from sources believed to be reliable,
but its accuracy and completeness, and the
opinions based thereon, are not guaranteed.